# LAND NAVIGATION

## Routefinding
with
## Map & Compass

BY WALLY KEAY

D1077737

**THE DUKE OF EDINBURGH'S AWARD**

Gulliver House, Madeira Walk, Windsor,
Berkshire SL4 1EU

**First edition May 1989**
**Second edition November 1995 (First Impression)**
**April 1999 (Second Impression)**

© Wallace Keay 1989
© The Duke of Edinburgh's Award

Printed in Great Britain by
Clifford Press Ltd., Coventry

Designed by Richard Brown FCSD

First edition ISBN 0 905425 06 5 (Paperback)
First edition ISBN 0 905425 05 7 (Hardback)
Second edition ISBN 0 319 00 845 Z

Every participant in the Bronze level of the Award Scheme has to take part in an Expedition of some sort. To qualify for the Silver and Gold Awards, there is a choice between an Expedition and an Exploration, but in every case it is essential to be able to navigate accurately in unfamiliar country. Failure means getting lost, with all the attendant risks and dangers, and causing anxiety to families and leaders.

This book sets out to explain the mysteries of the art of navigation on land for the benefit of instructors and participants so that they will be able to plan challenging expeditions and to undertake them in the confident knowledge that the chosen routes will be followed correctly.

I hope that the knowledge acquired from the study of this book will bring many happy and carefree hours travelling through beautiful countryside.

# CONTENTS

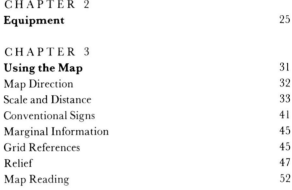

## PART 3
Mountain and
Wild Country
Navigation

**PART 4**
Extending Your
Skills

# FOREWORD

Although I am delighted, and honoured, to be asked to write the introduction to this book it is, in many ways, quite appropriate.

Navigator was the term applied to the labourers who excavated the network of Canals or "navigations" which was the main method of transporting raw materials, manufactured and farming produce up to the beginning of the nineteenth century. When the railways began to replace the canals the term navigator stuck—and is still with us today in the term "navvy" applied to those who build and repair our roads and motorways.

Those early navvies, however, had a distinct advantage over those of us who are learning to navigate with map and compass today. In fact they did not need some of the techniques, such as "aiming off" described in this book! If they came upon an obstacle in their path—such as a hill or a river—they simply dug a cutting or tunnel straight through it or built a bridge over it.

Today the railways play their part in assisting those who wish to learn to navigate by providing a possible means of travel to wild country areas, National Parks, to the start—and home again from the end—of long distance footpaths or even, with inter-rail links, to the remoter mountainous areas of Central Europe and Scandinavia.

I am delighted that British Rail, through our Community Unit, is able to sponsor this publication and trust that this book will help young people, and those not so young, travel into the beautiful countryside in confidence and safety.

Sir Robert Reid, CBE

# INTRODUCTION

If there is a core curriculum in outdoor pursuits and activities then surely finding one's way must be part of it, even if this only consists of finding the way to the location or venue and one's way back home. Unfortunately, navigation does not always receive the time, effort and attention which it deserves. This results in many people, especially a considerable number of the many tens of thousands of young people who participate in expeditions, getting lost, arriving late, tired and exhausted, and is also an on-going source of concern for those who are responsible for their supervision. Sadly those whose navigation is inadequate can never experience the deep sense of satisfaction, pleasure and freedom which comes from being able to navigate with confidence.

Navigation, especially in remote areas, is largely a matter of confidence and it is my hope that this book will supply the techniques which will engender that confidence and develop those latent talents which we all possess.

All books represent the efforts of many people and a book of this nature is more dependant than most for diagrams and illustrations to give added meaning to the text. I must thank Brian King and Nick Gair for transforming my sketches into the excellent illustrations without which the book would make much less sense and to Richard Brown for the design and colour work. My thanks also to those who have provided the photographs and in particular to Jim Gregson for his excellent mountain scenes, the Lake District National Park, Mike Blisset, Bill Marshall and Andreas Amling. My gratitude to Jack Ashworth, Peter Boulter, Bob Pettigrew, Tom Price and Brian Ware for their invaluable advice and, along with Gladys Field, for having the patience to read the text. I am also grateful for the availability of the resources of the Royal Geographical Society and to my daughter Jane and my son John for their support and patience while I have been engrossed in this task.

HRH The Prince Edward's Special Projects Committee has supplied the underlying support which has encouraged the expansion of the Award's literature. Above all, I am deeply grateful for the very special contribution made by the generosity of the British Rail Community Unit, and the support and interest of Sir Robert Reid, Trevor Toolan Managing Director, Personnel and James Crowe the Unit Manager, which has made this book possible.

There are plenty of books for the beginner on map reading; there are a few books which enable those who are already proficient navigators to find their way in the mountains, but there is a dearth of material for those in between. If this book, in some small way, helps to bridge this gap then my efforts, and the efforts of all concerned, will have been worthwhile.

Wallace Keay
May 1989

# PART 1

## MAP READING AND THE PREPARATORY SKILLS

# CHAPTER *1*

# HOW WE FIND OUR WAY

No conclusive experimental evidence has ever been produced to show that mankind has an innate sense of direction. There is no sixth sense which enables humans to find their way. Many migratory birds are equipped with a built-in navigation system which would do credit to a jumbo-jet. Recent research points to them even having back-up, or fail-safe systems which can be utilized when one method fails or is inadequate. When we compare ourselves with migratory birds and fishes we are ill-equipped to find our way and we will never be able to emulate the phenomenal navigation feats of the great shearwater, arctic tern, salmon or eel by our own unaided effort. But, like all the other mammals, we are able to find our way about with sufficient ease and confidence to meet our everyday needs and mankind is not designated homo sapiens without good reason. Though we lack the navigational endowment of many animals we can make good this deficiency by the application of intelligence and technology. Because we do not have the navigational ability of the homing pigeon or the turtle, it would be quite wrong to underestimate the navigational abilities with which we are all endowed.

For many thousands of years, people all over the world have been finding their way over great distances with a skill which appears positively uncanny. Mankind has colonized the earth from arctic waste to tropical rain forest and from desert to ocean island until he is the most widespread of all the mammals. Desert nomads have been able to cross trackless wastes while Polynesians made long ocean voyages in the Pacific without the use of the compass. This skill has always been based entirely on an acute awareness of the surrounding environment and a highly developed sensitivity towards nature—not a sixth sense, but the fullest use of all the existing five senses. Providing we clearly understand that we are not talking about a sixth sense, it is quite in order to speak of a sense of direction in the same way as we would speak of a sense of humour or a sense of gratitude. A sense of direction is not some mysterious gift which is bestowed on the chosen few; it is an ability which is acquired unconsciously or consciously. You have already acquired a sense of direction! The purpose of this book is to develop that sense of direction—with a little help from a map and a compass. Before attempting to do that it will be helpful to consider how we find our way.

There is a navigational hierarchy and it is not difficult to discern the major levels.

## The Visual Approach

From the moment we crawl, or take our first tottering steps we move towards somebody or something; mother, feeding-bottle or food. We can see something so we are able to travel towards it, even taking evading action on the way. This is so simple and obvious that it is easy to overlook the fact that it forms the basis of much of our route finding. No matter how sophisticated the methods of navigation which have been employed during the voyage of a supertanker or the flight of a passenger plane, the final approach is a visual one. If we can see our destination, whether it be the local Post Office or a distant mountain, we can make our way towards it. In horse racing this has given us the steeple-chase. If, on reaching our objective by visual means, we can see another objective which was not visible from our original starting place we can extend the distance of our travel. We can travel from one landmark to another, or from "point to point"—a method we all employ in everyday life. Stringing together a number of land or watermarks, which are visible from each other, gives the next highest form of navigation—pilotage.

## Pilotage

Though we tend to associate the word pilot with the aeroplane, let us not forget that a pilot was a person qualified by his local knowledge to take a ship in and out of harbour by steering from one mark to another. The word itself is derived from the Greek word for oar, which steered as well as propelled. The guides who have led traders, caravans and wagon-trains through wilderness country over the centuries have all used this principle. If, by the use of a map, we were able to select a number of landmarks, each one visible from the adjacent one, linking our starting point with our destination we

17

would have a very effective method of finding our way, even if the country between the start and the destination was completely unfamiliar.

## Map Memory

We are all endowed with "map memory". This has nothing to do with our ability to look at a map and commit the detail to memory. Map memory forms the basis of our daily movements around the localities in which we live and work. We gain this ability in the same way as other creatures, such as field mice or bees do, by travelling in different directions from our home base and gradually extending the distances. We build up a memory of the spatial relationship between all the different places and are then able to travel between them, even if they are out of sight, without the need to return to base first. Experiments have shown that bees actually have the capacity to make a "bee-line" between places a considerable distance apart without reference to the direction of the hive. We have all acquired this "map memory" without conscious effort though, it is true to say, it is more highly developed in some than in others. By conscious effort you will find that your ability can be greatly enhanced over a very short period.

## Travelling in a Preferred Direction

This is where we part company with the more able of the migratory creatures. We have no internal mechanism like a homing pigeon or a salmon which will enable us to travel on a course without reference to external landmarks. Fortunately we have been able to overcome our deficiency by technology—the Chinese invented the magnetic compass and provided us with a means of orienting ourselves without any external reference points or landmarks. For centuries sailors have been finding their way using compasses far less sophisticated than the ones we have at our disposal. All we need to do is develop our skill in the use of the instrument to the same high levels which they attained.

## Navigation

The highest level of navigation is the ability to find two places on a map, determine a course which will lead from one to the other and then be able to make that journey. This level of navigation assumes that we are able to use a map and other navigational instruments and have the ability to reason and apply the appropriate skills. It is hoped that you will be able to acquire these skills from this book, especially as we have some things working in our favour; at least the land on which we travel keeps still which is more than can be said for the sea under a ship, or the air surrounding an aircraft. This, and the fact that on land we are rarely blown off course, makes navigation considerably easier and eliminates all the complex mathematics and calculations; in fact we seldom need to do more than the simplest of additions and subtractions.

*"Compared with migratory birds we are ill-equipped to find our way".*

## How to Use the Book

The book is divided into four parts. Part 1 is concerned with skills of map reading; but only those skills which are essential for the purposes of route finding and your more obvious needs—all the rest have been eliminated; though you may find some back-up material in the appendices. These map reading skills are not navigational skills but the preparatory skills without which it would be difficult or impossible to find your way by the use of the map. You will be able to master these preparatory map reading skills indoors.

Part 2 is concerned with the basic skills of route finding. The foundation on which these skills rest is the ability to set, or orient, the map and being able to find your own position, or find your position and set the map. These basic skills can only be acquired out-of-doors by constantly comparing the map with the landscape or countryside. The acquisition of these basic skills should enable you to find your way through normal and open country; or that country which the Scouts and Guides so aptly call "green field country", with confidence. The third dimension, altitude, has been ignored. Not because it does not exist in this kind of country, steep climbs are to be found quite frequently, but because they are rarely prolonged as in mountainous areas and they do not usually have a serious navigational influence.

Part 3 is concerned with navigation in mountainous and wild country. The basic skills of Part 2 are developed further and the techniques required to deal with altitude are introduced. Emphasis is placed on the major landforms which can so influence the routes we take and on which we frequently have to rely to establish our location. Bad weather and restricted visibility are part of the mountain environment so Part 3 sees the introduction of the compass, but the techniques are limited to the three which are considered to be the most important. As in Part 2, every effort has been made to be selective and not over-saturate the reader with skills which are rarely used and frequently lead to confusion.

Part 4 is concerned with a description and appraisal of all the major or common skills and techniques involved in navigation on land which are based on the use of map and magnetic compass. The reader can pick and choose according to his needs and experience. Some of these techniques may be considered to be essential and the reader should decide on the appropriate time when they should be assimilated. It also considers the use of both the map and the compass in other parts of the world.

Each Part, and for that matter each chapter, is based on the previous parts or chapters. It is essential that the skills of one chapter are mastered before proceeding to the next. It is, however, impossible to acquire the skills of navigation just by reading a book. Understanding is not sufficient in itself. The skills have to be practised until they are part of you; able to stand up to all the stress and anxieties with which you may be faced in a desperate situation. By all means take the book in your pack, but always remember, you have to be taught by a stern and more persuasive teacher than myself—experience.

*"All who use the outdoors have a duty of care and protection".*

While every effort has been made to harmonize the various aspects of this subject, it is your responsibility to ensure that your skills and experience in mountaincraft progress in harmony with your navigational skills, for if either get out-of-step, you may well find yourself in serious trouble. Similarly, your personal clothing and equipment will have to be developed to take care of the increasing demands which will be placed upon them as it becomes necessary to practise the navigational skills in increasingly demanding terrain.

In addition to the responsibility of ensuring that your mountaincraft keeps pace with your navigational progress, you have the additional responsibility of caring for the countryside. All who use the outdoors have a duty of care and protection. This care entails not only a knowledge and observance of the Country Code but extends beyond this. Because so much of our route finding involves the use of paths, there is a particular responsibility to care for them and avoid any action or behaviour which would add to the serious erosion which so many of our more popular footpaths are suffering. Commonsense and forethought are required to avoid the unnecessary walking in line abreast or the thoughtless short cut. The stone walls, which should not be climbed, the gates and stiles which have involved so much craftsmanship and effort in their construction, must all receive the respect which is their due.

Your eyes are always your most important navigational instruments. Navigation is all about observation. Many of the navigational problems that groups of young people face in the hills and wild country arise out of their failure to observe. They are inward looking, concerned with themselves, their companions and their problems. They fail to give that attention to the detail of their surroundings and what is happening around them. For navigational purposes the ideal size of a party would be one, but common sense rules this out for the vast majority in most environments. It is important while learning to navigate that the size of the party is kept to the minimum consistent with safety and common practice. Ability will improve rapidly once you have gained sufficient experience to come to terms with travelling in a group and can devote the greater part of your attention to your surroundings.

The definition of normal or open and wild country used in this book is that used by The Duke of Edinburgh's Award and the Mountain-walking Leader Training Board. Scout and Guide "green field country" corresponds roughly with "normal and open country". There is a map at the back of the book with a list of the "wild country" areas. I have always resisted attempts to relate safety to a specific contour or height above sea-level. There is no height below which you are safe, or no particular height above which you are in danger—so much depends on experience and many factors which are beyond our control; weather conditions being the most obvious. It is possible, however, to discern a height in mainland Britain where there is a marked change in climate, where wind and rainfall increase and temperature falls with a marked influence on vegetation and a consequent change in land use; this change is most noticeable around the 200 and 250 metre contours and varies towards the western and eastern coasts.

The metrication of the longer units of linear measure proceeds at a snail's pace, if at all. Professional navigators will always use the nautical mile related to the circumference of the earth, one minute of a great circle through the earth's poles. The power and influence of the USA will ensure the survival of the imperial units, yards, feet and inches, not to mention the mile. We are conditioned by our road signs to think in terms of miles and yards for all outdoor measurements whichever units we use in the home, at work or school. Older readers will no doubt wish to continue using yards and miles, especially if, over the years, they have developed a strong sense of distance; it would be a shame to throw this ability away or try to metricate it. With the metrication of our maps, the use of international scales and especially since the metrication of contours, all who are in the process of acquiring the skills of finding their way on land should always think in metres and kilometres. The manipulation of numbers is so much easier from the decimalization and the maps condition you to think metrically. Older readers will find little difficulty in converting to imperial measure if they so wish and the word mile is used from time to time to reassure.

The language of the book is directed to the person on foot because they have a greater ability to reach the least accessible places on land. In catering for their needs it should be possible to meet the route finding needs of the person on a bicycle, horse-back, motor vehicle, or a canoe or boat on inland water. Practically all the skills and techniques are common to all forms of travel on land but here and there the reader may have to make an adjustment to the language.

You will have to practise. There is no such thing as instant navigation, crash courses only lead to crashes! The skills of navigation, like all the valuable skills in life, can only be acquired by the dedication of time and effort. But the rewards are great. Navigation is in itself a most enjoyable and challenging craft. When you come off the moor or hill and find your destination just below, you will be able to share in that deep sense of satisfaction enjoyed by sailors over the ages, when they make their landfall opposite the harbour entrance. Above all the ability to navigate will bring a wonderful sense of freedom. It lifts the burden of anxiety which afflicts and constrains all who are fearful of being lost.

# CHAPTER 2

## EQUIPMENT

## Maps

You will need two maps of the area in which you are going to learn to navigate. Ideally this area should be as near to where you are based as possible and, therefore, where you can spend the most time. If all the land is covered with buildings and roads it may become frustrating and it would be wiser to select maps which include some open country on the edge of town preferably with a maze of footpaths, easy access and not very far away. One map should be the 1:25000 scale "Pathfinder" series while the other should be the 1:50000 "Landranger" map of your locality. The 1:50000 map will be readily available in most good bookshops or stationers but you will probably need to visit your nearest Ordnance Survey map agent for the 1:25000 map. It is important that you do this because, of the two maps, the larger scale 1:25000 is by far the better map with which to learn to navigate, because it shows a lot more detail including field boundaries. You will need to become equally familiar with the 1:50000 scale maps. It is important to see how both maps depict the areas which you know well and interesting to compare and contrast the representation at the two different scales. Ensure that the maps are the latest editions and not old stock. As your navigational skills develop and you venture into more demanding terrain you will need other maps, but the section on Scale and Distance in Chapter 3 will provide additional advice on choosing your map. Notice carefully how your new maps have been folded so that you will be able to fold them in the same manner after use and prolong the life of the map.

It is possible to purchase the 1:50000 maps as flat sheets in addition to the more familiar folded form with the pink cover. It may be worthwhile purchasing the flat sheet of your local area from the O.S. stockist as it is less bulky and easier to fold to the selected area before fitting into your map case.

## Map Case

Your map will need protection from the elements if it is not to be prematurely recycled into wood pulp. Many experienced mountain walkers are quite content to use a plastic bag which has the advantage of costing little or nothing and enables the map to be tucked inside a jacket pocket; a distinct advantage for the climber or scrambler who will not wish to have anything dangling around the neck. Your needs are greater; you will need to spend many hours comparing map and country and this cannot be done if the map is hidden away inside a pocket. A proper map case is essential during the learning stage and these are available in Outdoor shops. Choose one which is sufficiently large to show a reasonable expanse of country at the 1:25000 scale (about 25 by 25 cm or 10 by 10 inches). It should have a strap or stout lanyard to attach itself to you, and the cover should be as robust as you can find. It is helpful, while learning to navigate, to make the map case more rigid by finding a sheet of thin, stiff plastic, such as a "Formica" off-cut, cutting it to size and inserting into the case. Your map case can then serve as your portable "chartroom table" and provide a firm base on which to work and one that will not be flapping about in the wind. In the outdoors a map case makes a map manageable!

It is possible to protect maps in other ways. They can be covered with transparent self-adhesive film—"tacky-back", available under a number of different trade names; this about doubles the price of the map. Outdoor Centres find this form of protection invaluable and cost effective where maps of a particular area are in constant use; for at least the maps can be wiped clean. For personal use, especially where the individual is intending to build up a collection of maps, it can have disadvantages. It adds significantly to the cost, makes the maps bulky and difficult to fold and eventually the film and the map crack at the folds. With some films the adhesive causes the orange dye of the contours to "bleed" over a period of time. Adhesive film makes the map bulky, hard to fold and insert into a map case, so it is difficult to use maps protected in this way with a map case.

It is also possible, with a little experimentation, to protect maps in other ways. There are proprietary brands of sprays and liquids for protecting wall paper which provide a cheap and effective way of protecting maps. Similarly, the silicon and wax based sprays used for water-proofing tents are very effective although some leave the map with a slightly waxy feel which one soon gets used to. It is of course, essential to protect both sides of the map with any of these sprays or liquids. Maps protected in this way are easily wiped clean with a damp cloth. It is possible to purchase commercially produced waterproof maps.

## Watch

If past experience is to be used effectively for planning future ventures, it is essential to know how long past journeys took and the speed of travel over differing kinds of terrain. Occasionally elapsed time may be the only indication of how far we have travelled and where we are located. The watch is therefore an important navigational instrument and only the map and the compass take precedence over it; generally the watch will be referred to scores of times for every time use is made of the compass. In the age of the disposable watch, when the cost of replacing the battery or cell may be more than the cost of buying another watch, the modern watch is incredibly accurate and excellent value for money. Many have a "stop-watch" facility which is a most useful additional feature.

## Compass

There is a wide variety of compasses available with an equally wide range of prices. The most useful is the protractor type compass which was developed for the orienteer. It is robust and simple to use and should meet all your future needs providing it has certain features. The needle should be in a liquid filled capsule to enable it to rotate freely and settle quickly and the housing should be transparent so that you can see through to the map underneath. The base plate should not be much less than 10 cm (4 inches) long. A cord will enable you to attach the compass to you or to your map case. It is doubtful if it is worth paying the additional price for the luminous variety as the marks on the common orienteering compasses are not usually large and bright enough for night work and it is necessary to find other solutions in the dark. A magnifying lens is an excellent feature, it focuses attention as well as the image.

## Light

A map is useful only as long as there is enough light for you to read it. In the dark, the time when you may need it most, it is reduced to just another piece of paper. All who go into the hills or venture off the beaten track should carry emergency lighting. You do not need much light to read a map, too much light may become detrimental by destroying your "night-sight". If the need is just to provide enough light to read the map then a Penlight will provide a cheap, lightweight and effective solution. If you are overtaken by darkness you may also need light to see where you are putting your feet and you will need a brighter light for this than reading the map, while those on expeditions may also need light around camp. Cells and batteries are heavy, so small and medium sized torches taking either a couple of AA, HP7, MN1500 or HP11, MN1400 size batteries represent a good compromise between saving weight and providing sufficient brightness. Though you may not need a very bright light you may need light over a prolonged period of time, especially during the months of the autumn, winter and spring. The most effective way of ensuring this is to use alkaline cells rather than zinc-carbon cells. These are more expensive initially but they do last 5 or 6 times longer than their zinc-carbon

*"1 : 25000 map shows the field boundaries—avoids problems with the landowner".*

equivalents and thus prove cheaper in the long run. The saving in weight is much more important as you would need at least five times the weight in zinc-carbon cells to provide light over the same period of time. Alkaline cells also have a much longer "shelf life" and reach you in better condition and are less likely to corrode and damage your torch than zinc-carbon cells. Because alkaline cells are so reliable there would seem to be little merit, at the present time, in purchasing the much more costly lithium cells which can also be unpredictable. Rechargeable cells such as Nicads also tend to be unpredictable unless they are regularly used and carefully maintained by those skilled in their care. Zinc-carbon cells have another disadvantage when compared with alkaline cells; they do not function when the temperature drops to around freezing point. This may not be important during the summer months but it can be a considerable disadvantage to the mountaineer or the winter navigator. All cells and batteries function better at higher temperatures so it can be a help to keep torches in the trouser pocket or inside the sleeping bag in very cold weather. A little extra life can usually be coaxed out of a dead cell by warming.

For those who use the outdoors at all seasons of the year, for campers and people intending to navigate at night, the cap or headlamp may be a worthwhile investment. It is more expensive than a hand torch but it has the important advantage of leaving the hands free.

## Other Items

A small, thin, note-book and a pencil, preferably a soft 2B, hexagonal, sharpened at both ends, more or less completes the essential equipment. You will need to measure distances on the map and a short length of thin string will be a cheap and effective way of doing this. You can also purchase a device for measuring distances on a map called an opisometer. See Chapter 3.

A romer and a simple measuring scale will be helpful but it is better and more instructive to make your own rather than purchasing these, and they will be dealt with in the appropriate chapters as will any items of a more specialized nature.

# THE PREPARATORY SKILLS

Using the map as an instrument of navigation is dependent on being able to "set" or orient the map and being able to relate the map to the countryside. This is the fundamental skill and can only be mastered by a great deal of practice out of doors. There are, however, a number of preparatory skills which are essential to becoming a competent map reader. Mastering these skills alone will not turn you into a navigator as they are purely map reading skills, but they will enable you to reach the starting gate. These preparatory skills can all be learnt indoors.

A map is simply an aerial picture, or representation, of the ground which shows all the important landmarks and features, such as hills, valleys, rivers, roads, footpaths and buildings, by means of signs and symbols. All the features are in the correct direction from each other and they are at the correct "scale distance" apart. Maps are reduced representations or pictures of the ground they represent, and the size of the reduction is the scale of the map. In this book the words ground, country, landscape or terrain will be used in the text and diagrams to denote the actual earth's surface on which we move and to differentiate this from the map.

## Map Direction

Navigation is about direction and maps give the direction of one place from another. Direction is best expressed in terms of the more important points of the compass, the 4 cardinal (North, East, South, West) and 4 half-cardinal (North East, South East, North West, South West) points. See Fig. 3.1. These eight directions are sufficient for all your needs. Just relate the direction of any two places to the nearest of these points but you can, if you wish, say that the direction of A from B is midway between two adjacent points. Where greater accuracy is required it is more convenient to express direction in terms of degrees.

The map itself provides direction; the top of the map is always the North, the bottom South, the right hand edge is the Easterly direction, while the left hand side indicates the West. Similarly the corners, or the diagonals, give the half-cardinal directions, North-East, South-East, North-West, South-West. See Fig. 3.2.

Whenever two places are considered the first and most important relationship which should be established is that of direction. Great care should always be placed on the use of the words "from" and "to", especially when communicating with others or you may well find yourself travelling in exactly the opposite and wrong direction.

**FIG. 3.1**  The principal directions

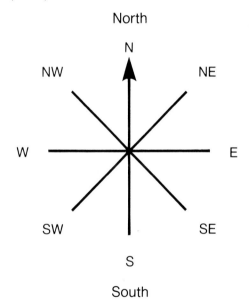

## Scale and distance

### Scale

Map scale is the most important factor in deciding which maps we use to find our way. The larger the scale of the map the more room there is to show detail and the easier it is to navigate with, but a price has to

**FIG. 3.2** Direction from the map

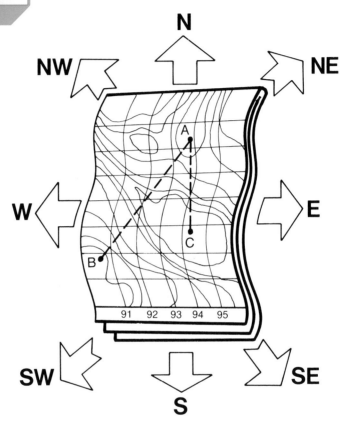

be paid for this convenience. The larger the scale, the more map, or maps, is needed to cover any given area of country. This obviously adds considerably to the cost of the maps and you may need to carry many more maps on your journey if it is over a considerable distance. If the scale of the map is too large you are continually "walking off the map". As a general rule, the faster you travel the smaller the scale of map required. Walkers tend to use 1:25000 and 1:50000 scale maps, while a cyclist would find a scale of a "Quarter of an inch to the mile" more convenient. A motorist will often use a map covering half the country.

Scale is expressed in three ways:

**1. In Words.** "Two and a half inches to the mile", "One inch to the mile", "Four centimetres to the kilometre". This is a very simple and easily understood way of expressing scale: a line four centimetres long on the map represents one kilometre of actual ground. Although, with the spread of metrication, this method of expressing scale is used less frequently.

**2. By a Representative Fraction or Ratio. "1:25000", "1:50000".** For example at a scale of 1:50000 one unit of length on the map represents 50000 of the same units on the ground, one centimetre on the map represents 50000 centimetres on the ground, or more practically two centimetres on the map represent one kilometre on the ground. With the metrication of our maps this method of expressing scale has become much more widespread as the two maps which dominate the outdoor scene are at a scale of 1:25000, or 4 cm to the kilometre (approximately two and a half inches to the mile) and 1:50000, 2 cm to the kilometre (approximately one and a quarter inches to the mile); they are referred to by their representative fractions: "one to twenty-five thousand" or "one to fifty thousand". Always remember that the larger the ratio, the smaller the scale of the map. The 1:50000 map, where 2 centimetres (cm) represents 1 kilometre (km) of ground, is a smaller scale map than the 1:25000 where 4 cm on the map represents 1 km on the ground.

**3. By a Scale Line.** This is a visual, practical and simple way of showing scale. It does not require any arithmetical ability or the manipulation of numbers. Scale lines are drawn on the margins of the map in the most frequently used units, kilometres and fractions of a kilometre, miles and fractions of a mile. While this is the most practical method of depicting scale for the navigator, it is of no use for verbally describing the scale of maps.

**Choice of Scale.** Two maps are of overwhelming importance to those involved in the outdoors in Great Britain; the Ordnance Survey's 1:50000 *Landranger Series* and their 1:25000 *Pathfinder* and *Outdoor*

*Leisure Series.* All who wish to become proficient in route finding must be capable of using both of these scales with equal ease. The larger scale 1:25000 map with its greater detail is the better map with which to learn to navigate. 1:25000 maps are available for all of England, Scotland and Wales and every effort should be made to obtain one of your own locality as it will make your task much easier. There is only one 1:25000 map in Northern Ireland at present, the Mournes, but the whole of Ulster is covered at the 1:50000 scale, as is most of Europe. If it is impossible to obtain a 1:25000 scale map use a 1:50000 as all the skills and techniques are identical; it is usually just that little bit harder to apply them.

© *Crown copyright*

**FIG. 3.3** Comparison of scales

1:50000          1:25000

The 1:25000 being twice the scale provides four times the area to show more detail and, in particular, the field boundaries. The extra detail makes route-finding easier, enables the correct path to be found and followed and reduces the possibility of friction with the landowner.

Looking at Fig. 3.3 you see that by doubling the scale of the map there is four times as much area in which to show detail, thereby providing a much clearer representation of the ground, which is the first great advantage of the larger scale. The larger scale also enables field boundaries to be shown. Looking again at the 1:50000 map in Fig. 3.3 it gives the impression of openness, tempting one to consider a route leading off to either side: comparison with the 1:25000 immediately shows that the area is covered with small fields or meadows and deviation from the track is out of the question. This is the other great advantage of the 1:25000 scale map, it enables more realistic routes to be planned, reduces the problems over access to land and makes for happier relations with the people who live and work in the countryside.

## Distance

If direction is the first and most important relationship which the navigator has to establish between any two places, the second most important is distance. It is vital to be able to measure the distance between two places on the map quickly and accurately. Rarely, except in open country or moorland, is this in a straight line or "as the crow flies". It nearly always involves measuring around the twists and turns of tracks and footpaths. The most usual method is to take a piece of thin string and lay it carefully along the road or paths which form the chosen route and then lay it straight along the scale line on the margin

**FIG. 3.4** Lay string or edge of paper along route

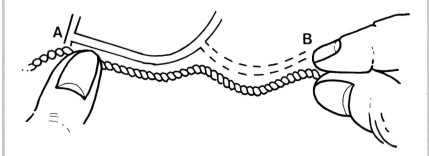

**FIG. 3.5** Use linear scale on map

Fractions of a unit to the left of zero

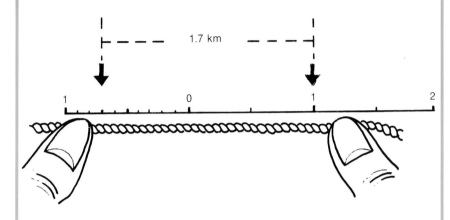

1.7 km

of the map. See Fig. 3.4. There are usually two scale lines, a metric one in kilometres and metres, and one in Imperial Measure, miles and parts of mile or yards. Note carefully where the zero is on the scale ; to the right of the zero are whole units while to the left are the smaller divisions or fractions. By positioning one end of the string on the scale line at the appropriate whole unit to the right of zero, it is possible to read off the distance accurately from the smaller fractions to the left of the zero. See Fig. 3.5.

Instead of using a piece of thin string it is possible to use the same technique with the straight edge of a piece of paper, marking the paper at each sharp turn and then laying it along the scale line.

## A Measuring Scale

As an alternative to following the route with the edge of a piece of paper it is possible to construct a measuring scale out of a piece of card and read off the distance directly instead of having to make use of the linear scale on the margin of the map. With a little practice it is possible to become very adept at measuring distances in a matter of seconds with far less chance of error than using the scale on the map or the measure on your compass. Appendix 1 will show you how to use such a scale for both the 1 : 25000 and the 1 : 50000 scale maps.

As well as needing the ability to measure distances quickly and accurately on the map, it is also helpful to be able to estimate distances by the eye alone. The grid lines being spaced at 4 cm and 2 cm on the 1:25000 and 1:50000 respectively, and representing 1 kilometre of actual countryside are a great help. The diagonal distance across a square of grid is about 1.5 kilometres. Practise measuring distances with string, paper and your measure until you are proficient, even over intricate routes; but before you measure the distance between two places always estimate the distance first by the eye alone, in a direct line as well as along your chosen route.

*"Manmade line features are just as important for indicating direction".*

## Commercial Map Measurers

As mentioned in the previous chapter it is possible to purchase an instrument called an opisometer for measuring distances on a map. Choose one with a straight shaft as they are easier to twirl between the finger and thumb when following the route. Make sure that the needle on the dial is at zero, then trundle it along the route you wish to measure. At some scales it is possible to read the distance directly off the dial but usually it is necessary to trundle them in the opposite direction along the scale on the edge of the map. With experience in manipulation opisometers can be used very effectively and they can be a great help in speeding up route planning.

# Distance and Time

Measuring distance on the map is only a means to an end. The real purpose is to determine how long it will take to get from one place to another or to find out how long a journey will take. If we know how long a journey will take we can add it to our time of departure and estimate our time of arrival at our destination: an Estimated Time of Arrival or ETA. Unlike the pilot of an aeroplane or the captain of a ship we cannot determine our economical cruising speed in advance and we will need some practical experience before we can make reliable estimations of our speed of travel over various types of terrain.

*"—the purpose is to determine how long it will take to get there".*

## Conventional Signs

Conventional Signs are the shorthand of the map maker. These signs and symbols are used to convey much of the information without obscuring or cluttering up the map. They become familiar with constant use but every time you meet one which you do not know look it up in the Legend or Key on the margins of the map. Very few people extract from the map more than a fraction of the information which the map maker has provided. Pay particular attention to signs which may cause confusion, for example on the 1:25000 map, a footpath without a right-of-way is easy to differentiate from a Parish Boundary when you can compare them on the key but less easy when they are viewed in isolation on the map. Compare the symbols on your 1:50000 map with those on your 1:25000 because you should be able to change from one to the other without confusion. Compare a Path without a right of way on the 1:50000 with the County, Borough or Constituency Boundary on the 1:25000 scale.

The Conventional Signs are grouped into logical and helpful categories which makes for easy reference but, for your navigational needs, it is helpful to form the habit of always dividing them into three groups based on their relevance to your route finding needs.

*"Spot features enable you to pinpoint your location accurately".*

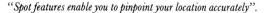

41

*"Line features provide direction, and often a route as well".*

## 1. Point or Spot Features

Into this group place all the signs and symbols which represent particular places, so that they can pinpoint a location and enable you to establish where you are. Churches with spires or towers, all buildings, mile stones or posts, television or radio masts, bridges, towers and tall chimneys are all obvious landmarks. Some features may be quite extensive, such as a quarry or a spoil heap, but even these may help you to locate yourself to within a hundred metres or so.

## 2. Line or Linear Features

This category should include all the features which have length: roads, paths, rivers, electricity transmission lines and the less obvious features such as field boundaries. Because they have length they also have direction, even a river meandering over its flood plain has a general direction, and their direction can, in turn, provide you with direction. Some line features, such as a field boundary, may be less than a hundred metres long while a river or a road may be measured in hundreds of kilometres. These major features may change direction very markedly and frequently form great arcs but nevertheless they have orientation which is important. See Fig. 3.6.

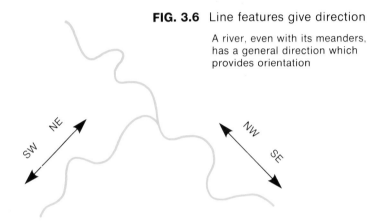

**FIG. 3.6** Line features give direction

A river, even with its meanders, has a general direction which provides orientation

## 3. Area Features

The signs in the first group mark a place and will enable us to pin-point our position, while those in the second group have length which may give us direction or something to aim at if we are lost. In the third group we place all the features which have area. These are principally concerned with types of terrain and vegetation. Obvious examples are woods, forests, scrub, sand dunes, mud flats, marshes, scree, and boulder strewn land. These features may be of help in determining where we are, but, more importantly, they all have a considerable influence on our speed of travel.

Try and place all the Conventional Signs into one of these three categories. Some may not fit and, occasionally, you may not know in which group to place a feature, but always try. Features which are not actually discernible on the ground, such as a County Boundary, should obviously be ignored as they cannot be of any assistance in route finding.

*"Area features may have a considerable influence on our speed of travel".*

## Marginal Information

In addition to the key to the Conventional Signs and the linear scales mentioned earlier, there is other very important information on the borders of a map. There will be a date, or dates, stating when the map was compiled and/or revised, and possibly the dates of the surveys from which the compilation was made. Some features on a map must inevitably become out of date just after the survey has been completed and before the map is even printed. This is especially so around our ever expanding towns and cities. Maps of urban areas are revised more frequently to cope with these changes but changes do occur all over the country. New features appear while others disappear; the camp site you were anticipating may have been replaced by a four star hotel, while the bothy where you intended to spend the night may have sunk without trace beneath a reservoir. Pay particular attention to the date on your map for it may help to account for many surprises and avoid much confusion. Information on the adjoining sheets and the National Grid is helpful. Information relating to North and magnetic variation will be dealt with in the appropriate chapter.

## Grid References

Grid References are not a great deal of assistance in helping you to find your way around the countryside. Historically speaking they are newcomers as features on civil maps. But they are an important means of communication. It is essential to be able to refer to a place on a map precisely and communicate its position quickly and accurately. The National Grid Reference System enables us to do this. A six figure Grid Reference will meet all your navigational needs. Maps are covered with blue grid lines running North/South called "Eastings" and lines running East/West called "Northings". These are spaced at 4 cm and 2 cm apart on the 1:25000 and 1:50000 scale maps respectively so that the distance between them always represents 1 kilometre of actual country. Each line is identified by two figures ranging from 00 to 99. In a six figure Grid Reference, the first three figures indicate how far to the East the place is while the second three figures show how far North the position is. The first two figures in each group of three are read from the map while the third figure is estimated

45

or measured. If you remember that the letter "E" comes before the letter "N" in the alphabet you will have no difficulty in remembering that "Eastings" come before "Northings". "Along the corridor and up the stairs" is also used as an aid to memory but there is always someone who cannot remember whether to go up the stairs first or along the corridor. East then North! See Fig. 3.7.

**FIG. 3.7** Grid references.

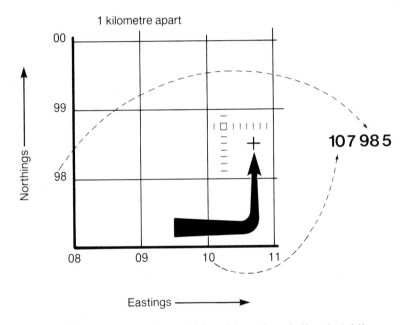

As the grid lines are numbered 00 to 99 and each line is 1 kilometre apart a six figure Grid Reference used without further qualification will be repeated every 100 kilometres (about 62 miles) but this does not cause any confusion in practice. In a later chapter we will examine Grid References in greater detail and see how to make them unique. A six figure Grid Reference locates a place to within 100 metres. There is an instrument called a Romer which can be used for measuring Grid References accurately; they can be purchased but it is much cheaper and far more instructive to make your own. This can

be added to the distance scale already mentioned and the details are given in Appendix 1. Find some point features on your map and work out their Grid Reference; practise this until you can do it quickly and accurately. Then do the opposite; ask someone to give you some references and find out where they are. If you have no one to do this for you, pick six figures at random within the range of Eastings and Northings on your map and see where it takes you. Practise until you are competent. Obviously the reference will apply to your 1:25000 or your 1:50000 map. If you have made yourself a Romer, or are using the one supplied with this book, always estimate the Grid Reference by the eye before measuring.

# Relief

The height, the shape, the landforms and the steepness of the ground are shown on the map by means of contours. To be able to visualize the shape and nature of the landscape from the contours of a map may take many years of constant practice, but you will be able to acquire the three most important skills with little difficulty. These three skills are:

■ Find the height of a place.
■ Appreciate the steepness of a slope.
■ Recognize a few of the major landforms such as a hill, valley, spur, ridge, and high and low flat ground.

These skills alone will more than meet the needs of all who find their way in normal or open country. Those who intend to venture into mountainous or wilderness country must know more about relief and contours, but they need to start here with the basics.

## Contours

A contour is a line drawn on a map joining all the places the same height above sea level. The difference in height between two successive contours is known as the vertical, or contour, interval. On 1:25000 maps the contours are at intervals of 5 metres in lowland areas and at 10 metre intervals in the upland areas. The contours are all at 10 metre intervals on the 1:50000 *Landranger* maps. Until the process of metrication is complete in the 1990's, many maps will continue to

47

be produced with the contour intervals based on imperial units but expressed in metres. There are still 1 : 25000 maps in circulation with the contours and heights expressed in feet. Every fifth contour is thickened to make it easier to follow, count and read. The numbers always read "up-hill". See Figs. 3.8, 3.9 and 3.10.

If you are using a different scale map or maps of a different country, the contour interval will almost certainly be found in the marginal information. All the procedures are the same.

**FIG. 3.8**  Contours.

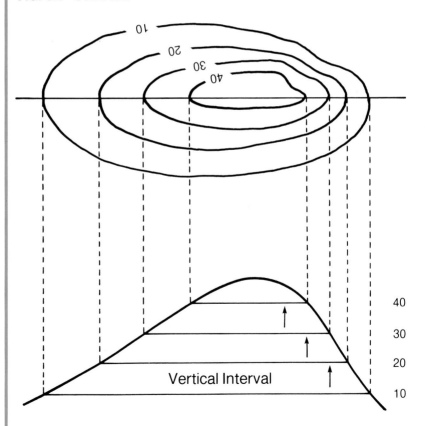

**FIGS. 3.9 & 3.10** Contours read "up-hill".

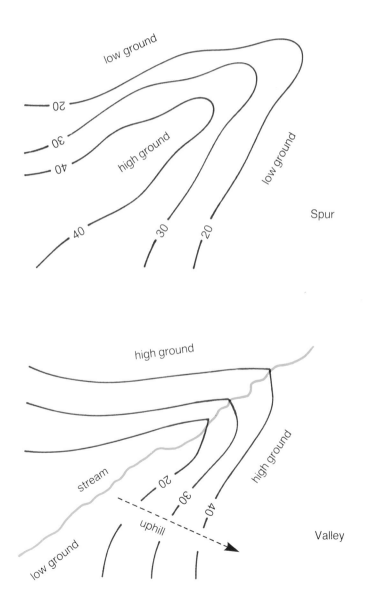

49

## Height

The ability to find the height of a place or, more usually, to be able to find the difference in height between two locations, is the third most important relationship to be established between two places after direction and distance. On the map, see Fig. 3.11, the farm at X is situated on a contour. By tracing the contour across the map, aided by the thicker contour, we can read off the height of the farm: 160 metres above sea level. Sometimes the contours have to be followed for a considerable distance before a number can be found to identify the height of the contour. For navigational purposes the height of the nearest contour to the place in question is sufficient for our needs, but it is usually reasonable to assume that if a place is situated halfway between two contours then its height lies half way between the contours. In Fig. 3.11 the building at Y is midway between the 140 and 150 metre contours so we can assume that its height is 145 metres.

**FIG. 3.11** Height from contours.

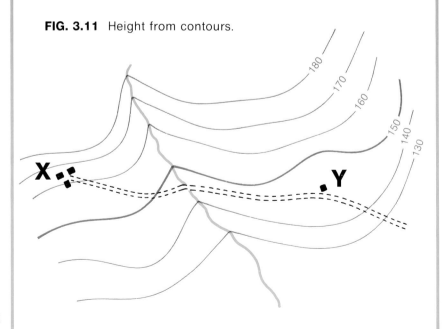

## Steepness of Slope or Gradient

The closer the contours are together the steeper the ground must be. Flat land, whether it is high or low will have few, if any, contours. You can form an impression of how steep a slope is by how tightly the contours are packed together and from the "orangey" colour of the map. But this impression from the map alone will have little meaning for the novice until it has been translated by a great deal of practical experience. Later, by counting the number of contours per cm of map and comparing it with the country over which you are walking, you will soon be able to appreciate the steepness of slopes from the map.

## Landforms

In order to plan sensible and satisfying routes, as well as to enable you to find your way around the countryside, you will need to be able to recognize certain common landforms from the map such as hills, valleys, spurs and ridges. There are many others which will concern you when we go into mountainous country but these will do to start with. All these landforms have characteristic shapes when represented by contours on a map. By constantly comparing map and landscape

*"All these landforms are represented by characteristic contour patterns".*

51

you will soon become familiar with them and learn to recognize them instantly. Fig. 3.8 shows the basic representation of a hill. In this particular example the eastern slope is steeper than that on the western side. In Figs. 3.9 and 3.10 the contours depicting a spur—high ground projecting into low ground—have a resemblance to those of a valley—low ground between higher ground—so it is important to look at the contour heights. Usually, but not always, valleys have the blue line of a stream or river running through them.

## Map Reading

So far we have considered a number of aspects of map reading, direction, scale, distance, conventional signs and contours as isolated skills. These skills must now be brought together and blended into the art of map reading. Maps have an endless variety of uses and all kinds of information may be stored and extracted from them; our map reading needs are limited to those concerned with route finding.

Look at Fig 3.12 and assume that we wish to travel from the Post Office at A to a campsite at the Quarry B. From the map it is possible to give the following description of the journey:

General Direction NE
Distance 2.4 kilometres.
"I shall turn left outside the Post Office, towards the East and along the village main street. After 200 metres there will be a church on my left and after another 100 metres a cross roads. I shall go straight on at the cross roads and the road will descend a hill and veer to the right. After a sharp left hand bend I will cross a bridge over a stream or river. The road will turn to the North and ascend the other side of the valley. On my left, the North-West side of the road, there will be a wood. 200 metres beyond the start of the wood the secondary road will turn to the East but I will continue straight ahead towards the North-East along an unmetalled road or track. After 300 metres, an unfenced track on my right will lead to some buildings, probably a farm. The unmetalled track or road will continue with a gradually increasing gradient for a further 300 metres until it reaches a quarry in a hillside and my campsite."

**FIG. 3.12** Map reading

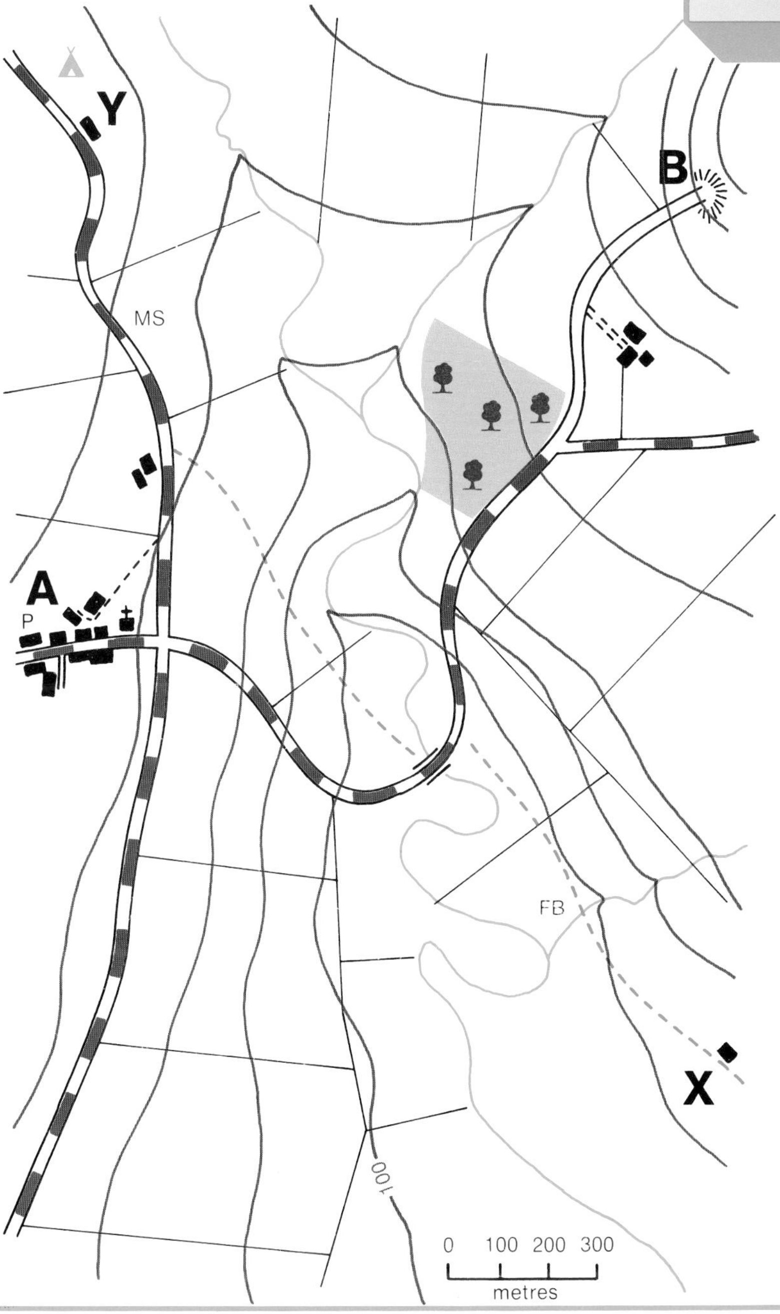

Y

B

MS

A

P

X

FB

0 100 200 300
metres

100

53

The first thing to note is that it is personalized. Once you are able to map read it is possible to describe a journey between two places on the map as if you were actually travelling along the route. You will be able to think of features as being "on my left", or "straight on". The first concern is with direction in terms of the cardinal and half-cardinal points. Because routes on land twist and turn the general direction, though very important, is sufficient for our needs when we are finding our way by the map.

After direction comes distance; the total distance along the route has been measured as well as the distance between certain landmarks. These distances are a means to an end, for later on you will be able, by practical experience, to translate these distances into travelling times. The 2.4 kilometres may be turned into a 25 minute walk.

Notice also how emphasis is placed on the landmarks on the route, primarily to ensure that we are on the correct route and secondly to keep track of our progress along the route.

More detail could have been given in the description; from the Conventional Signs we know that the church has a tower and that the wood is deciduous. If the route was longer it might be necessary to omit some of the detail. The amount of detail given in such a verbal description is not important. It is important that we are able to extract from the map all the detail that the map maker has provided when the need arises to enable us to find our way. Beware of making assumptions from the map; the buildings at the end of the unfenced track are in all probability a farm; past experience may lead us to this conclusion, but it could be something else. Draw on past experience but always keep an open mind.

The experienced map reader is able to carry out this process subconsciously but there is a considerable benefit in being able to describe such journeys in words. Write down a description of a journey from X to Y in Fig. 3.12.

Practise this skill until it becomes second nature. Write down

*"We know that the church has a tower and that the wood is deciduous".*

descriptions of various routes between places on your map using your own words. Later, in the outdoors, think about your routes in the same terms and words that are being used now. When you are a competent map reader you will be able to take a map of unknown terrain at the opposite end of the country, or the opposite side of the world for that matter, plan a route with all the essential navigational detail and landmarks. You will be able to visualize the sequence of their appearance. As your practical experience broadens to include different types of terrain and country, so you will be more able to fill in the background to your map reading with mental images which are all part of the delight and satisfaction of maps and map reading.

55

SUMMARY

This chapter has been concerned with mastering six preparatory skills of map reading:

Direction from the map.
Scale and distance.
Conventional Signs and the need to divide them into point, line and area features.
Marginal information.
Grid References.
Relief—height, gradient and a few basic landforms.

The first relationship to establish between two places is direction, distance is the second followed by the principal landmarks on the route.

Once these individual skills have been mastered they have to be unified into the ability to "map read"—to enable you to visualize and describe in navigational terms, a journey, or route, through unfamiliar country. When you are able to do this you are well on the way to being a competent map reader and should be able to face the outdoors with confidence.

# PART 2

## THE ESSENTIALS OF ROUTE FINDING IN NORMAL, OPEN OR GREENFIELD COUNTRY

# CHAPTER 4

## FINDING YOUR WAY
## IN NORMAL OR
## OPEN COUNTRY

The previous Chapter was concerned with the skills of map reading, but they are only a preparation for route finding and do little more than turn you into an armchair map reader. Route finding is a practical skill which can only be learnt out-of-doors by spending many hours comparing map with country and country with map.

The time has now arrived when it is essential to go out of doors. If you have any choice in the matter choose a warm day or wrap up warmly, for your first ventures into practical route finding will involve spending a great deal of time standing around and looking about. The ability to navigate is acquired through the use of the mind and not through the use of the legs, even though it will entail a great deal of walking and travelling in the future.

Fold your map so that the location where you are going to do your map reading is centred in the middle of the area of map and then place the folded map in the map case. Find your place on the map; it should be a familiar area—it could be outside your own doorstep.

## Locating Your Position

Take your 1:25000 map of the area where you are based. Find your home, your work place, school, village shop or supermarket on the map. Repeat this for several places which are familiar to you. Then think out how you did it. Did your eye fall on the location by chance? Did you scan the map systematically? Did you puzzle it out and which clues led to success? How important were the names on the map. Did you first find the locality by name and then gradually "home in" using roads and public buildings? The ability to locate your position on the map is fundamental to your success in finding your way. We locate our position by comparing the landscape or country with its representation on the map by the signs and symbols. This is easy in familiar and built-up areas, but it will be much more difficult in unfamiliar and featureless terrain. You must practise this skill in familiar terrain until it becomes second nature like the other basic skill of setting the map. Sometimes you will locate your position and then set your map while at other times setting the map first may help

**FIG. 4.1** Setting map by line feature.

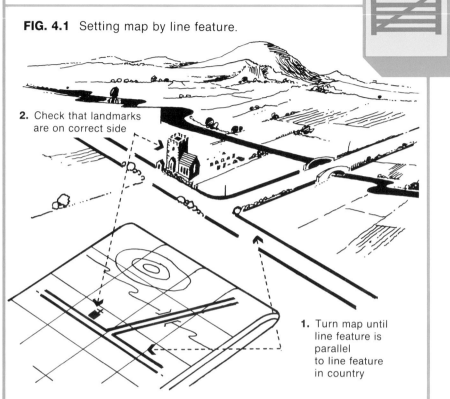

**2.** Check that landmarks are on correct side

**1.** Turn map until line feature is parallel to line feature in country

you to find your position, until hopefully, there will come a time when you will carry out the two processes at the same time. The difference between being lost and knowing where you are nearly always rests on your ability to place a finger on the map and say, "I am here!" This book is largely concerned with enabling you to place your finger on the map and point to your position, or at least your general whereabouts, for when you are able to do this you know your relationship with other places on the map and may plan a route to your destination.

## Setting the Map

Setting, orienting or orientating (see Glossary), the map is the fundamental skill in using the map for route finding. There are two common methods of setting the map by inspection and both should be practised until they become automatic.

61

## Method 1

### By a Line Feature

Look around the landscape and find a line or linear feature such as a street, road, path, ridge, river, boundary fence or wall—anything which has length and direction and which is marked on your map. Holding the map horizontally, turn your map round until the feature on the map is parallel with the feature on the ground. Your map should now be correctly set or oriented and all the other landmarks and features should be in the correct direction from the map. It is a very simple, quick and effective method and you do not need to know exactly where you are providing you have a rough idea of the area you are in. However it is possible to have the map exactly the wrong way round if you are not careful, so check that landmarks are on the correct side of the linear feature you selected. It is easy to practise this method anywhere, at home, at work or at school. Fig. 4.1

## Method 2

### By a Landmark or Point Feature

To use this method you must know where you are. Find your position on the map. Look around the landscape and find a spot feature which is marked on your map. Lay your pencil, or a straight-edge, through your position on the map and the spot feature on the map, and then, holding the map horizontally turn the whole map round until you can sight along the straight-edge from your position on the map, through the spot feature on the map to the feature on the ground. Your map is now correctly set. If you know your exact position this is a very accurate method of setting the map, but it will work quite effectively even if you only know your approximate position, providing you choose a spot feature which is some distance away. Fig. 4.2.

Put a map or street plan in your pocket when you go out—to the office, school, work or even taking the dog for a stroll, and keep on setting the map. After a while you will find that you can use line features which are further and further away. You will be able to find a couple of spot features and imagine a line joining them, converting

**FIG. 4.2** Setting map by point feature or landmark

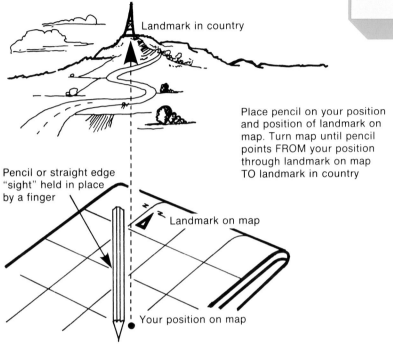

Landmark in country

Place pencil on your position and position of landmark on map. Turn map until pencil points FROM your position through landmark on map TO landmark in country

Pencil or straight edge "sight" held in place by a finger

Landmark on map

Your position on map

You must know where you are or your approximate position

them into a line feature! Place your pencil through the symbols of the features on the map and then rotate the map until it is parallel to the features on the ground. Eventually you will be able to set the map instinctively by just relating features shown on the map to those on the ground. When you find that you are setting the map without thinking how you are doing it, or by which method you are using—congratulate yourself for you now know how to set a map! There are other ways of setting a map—you could use your compass—but to have to use a compass, in good visibility in normal or open country with a surfeit of landmarks, is an admission of failure. Moreover, it would deprive you of the necessity to continually compare map and landscape which is the basis of all sound land navigation. Sometimes you will find it easier to set the map first and then locate your position but with experience you will find that you are usually carrying out both fundamental processes at the same time. You must become accustomed to looking

63

at your map with the words upside down or sideways on, so that eventually there is no "right way round" and to view it from any angle is normal.

## A Different Point of View

Before you can take full advantage of your ability to set the map, there may be a problem to overcome which could necessitate you making a series of journeys or visits. A map represents an aerial view of the ground—a bird's eye view or that of a person in an aeroplane—which is very different from our ground level view point. There will be many occasions when you literally will not be able to "see the wood for the trees" or even beyond the nearest hedge. This is something which you will have to come to terms with, but you can speed up this process and extend your skills at the same time. You will need to find a "vantage point"—the nearest hill or ridge to where you are based which will enable you to overlook a stretch of the landscape. Looking down from this point the terrain will have a more map-like appearance and you will be able to relate it to the map much more easily. The perspective will still be a little foreshortened but it will be better than at ground level. Even on plains and in lowland areas it is usually possible to find such a vantage point. It is certainly worth making a considerable effort to travel to such a place. If you live in a part of the country like the fens then there may be an alternative—if there are no high natural features it may be possible to use the view from an upper floor of a tall building or a tower. Again, it may take some effort to gain access but the benefits will make the effort worth while.

Having reached your vantage point, locate your position on the map and set the map using the second method (by a point feature). By now you will have realized that finding your position on the map and setting the map is often a "chicken and egg" situation—you do not always know which comes first. Sometimes you locate your position on the map and then set the map, while at other times setting the map assists you in finding your position. You should be used to looking at the map from all directions. With your map set a great deal of information becomes available and you can carry out a series of tasks.

**FIG. 4.3** A vantage point

A high viewpoint helps to give the country a
more maplike appearance and is especially
helpful to the novice

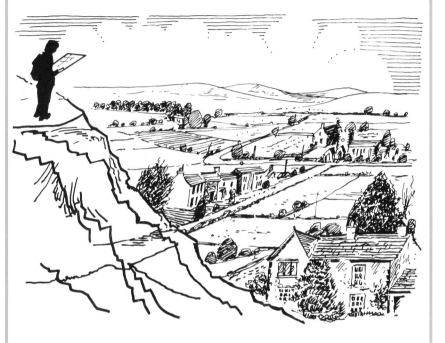

## Geographical Direction

You can determine direction in the landscape; you can look towards
the horizon in a certain direction and know that you are looking
North or South-West or whatever point you choose. In the previous
Chapter on Map Reading, direction was the first to be considered;
similarly in this section dealing with the practical skills, direction is
again the first consideration. We know that, by convention, North is
always at the top of the map, so by keeping the map set and looking
along the grid lines towards the top of the map we can look towards
the horizon and know that we are looking towards the geographic
North. Similarly we can look along the grid lines running across the
map towards the right-hand side and know that they are pointing
towards the East. A pencil laid across the diagonals of the grid and
pointing towards the bottom left hand corner of the map would point
South West. Fig. 4.3.

**FIG. 4.4** Using set map to point direction of travel

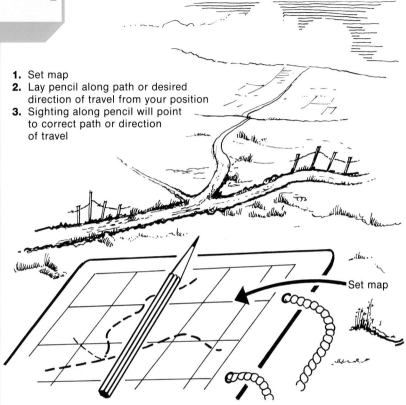

1. Set map
2. Lay pencil along path or desired direction of travel from your position
3. Sighting along pencil will point to correct path or direction of travel

Set map

## Route Direction

Just as it is possible to find direction in terms of the cardinal and half-cardinal points from an oriented map, so it is possible to use the set map to point out the direction in which to travel to reach your destination or check the direction of a road or path. Using the map "to point direction" is usually the most important function of a set map. Fig. 4.4.

The map is set, a pencil or straight edge is laid along the route to your objective, or the path you wish to use, from your position on the map. Keeping the map set, hold it in front of you and look along the pencil from your position end towards the objective. The pencil will now point the direction to take or point along the path. This technique is the basis of route finding with the map.

*"Keeping the map set sight carefully along a pencil".*

## Locating a Feature

One of the most useful techniques made possible by setting the map is to locate a landmark or feature shown on the map in the landscape. Keeping the map set, lay your pencil or straight edge through your position on the map and the symbol of the feature you wish to locate in the landscape. Then sight carefully along the pencil from your position end to the ground; the feature you are trying to locate will lie along the line of sight. When you are locating a feature you are working from MAP TO GROUND. Fig. 4.5.

67

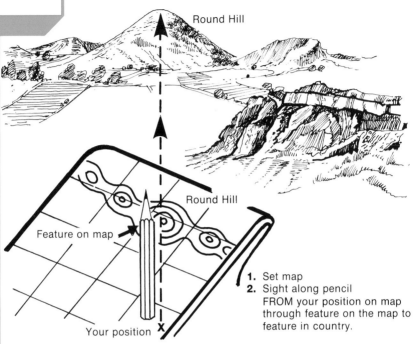

**FIG. 4.5** Locating feature in the country (Map to country)

Round Hill

Round Hill

Feature on map

1. Set map
2. Sight along pencil
   FROM your position on map
   through feature on the map to
   feature in country.

Your position X

## Identifying a Feature

The opposite technique to the previous one is when you wish to identify, or name, a feature which you can see in the landscape; it may be anything from a prominent hill to a village. With the map set, place one end of your pencil through your position on the map, swing it across the map until it is pointing to the feature on the ground. The feature, with its name or symbol, should be found along the pencil or straight edge providing that it is not too far away and is shown on the map. When identifying a feature in the landscape you are working from GROUND TO MAP. Fig. 4.6.

All these skills should be practised until they can be carried out without thinking. After a time you will become so confident that you will frequently be able to locate and identify features by sighting across the map with the eye alone. As with setting the map, it is the constant relating and comparison of map and ground which is forming the sound base for your navigational techniques.

**FIG. 4.6** Identifying a feature (Country to map)

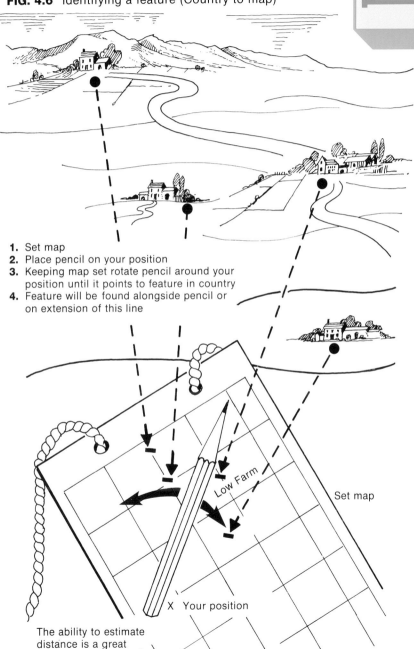

1. Set map
2. Place pencil on your position
3. Keeping map set rotate pencil around your position until it points to feature in country
4. Feature will be found alongside pencil or on extension of this line

Low Farm

Set map

X  Your position

The ability to estimate distance is a great help

## Route Finding

The overwhelming proportion of all outdoor travel takes place on roads, tracks and footpaths. Even in mountainous and wild country in the British Isles, probably about 90% of our movement takes place on paths. This is principally because where we go is largely determined by rights of way, problems of access, and access points. If you wish to walk to the top of Snowdon, the number of obvious departure points available to the public is limited and generations of hill walkers have already beaten a track to the top for you! This situation makes route finding much easier. The presence of a path or road usually solves the problem of direction, as it generally holds us on course as effectively as railway lines keep a train on its correct route. Our task is usually confined to following our progress along the path until we reach our destination or the point of departure for another path. There is an added advantage to the use of paths, for it enables us to acquire the fundamental techniques of route finding with the support of what the orienteers would call a "handrail" before we have to tackle the more difficult problems of mountain navigation or of trackless and featureless wild country.

*"Identify features marked on your map to pinpoint your position".*

In future we will use the word PATH to mean any footpath, track, bridleway or road—any of those features which exist on the ground and which are marked on the map. The use of the word FOOTPATH will be confined to a path which is intended for pedestrians, or where the use is limited to those on foot.

Route finding in normal or open country involves:

(**a**) Selecting a path, or paths, from the map which will enable you to reach your destination or achieve the purpose of your journey.

(**b**) Selecting landmarks or features along the paths from the map which will enable you to ensure that you are on the right path, and enable you to follow your progress along the path.

Using landmarks or features, common to both map and ground, to identify one's exact position is known as PINPOINTING one's position. Orienteers would refer to this process as "thumbing".

Following one's progress across the countryside on the map, by means of pinpointing, we will refer to as TRACKING one's position.

The purpose in acquiring the individual preparatory skills, and bringing them all together as "map reading" in Part 1, was to enable us to perform the techniques listed above. If you have made the effort to become a competent map reader you will have very few problems in their practical application.

Take your 1:25000 *Pathfinder* or *Outdoor Leisure Map* and select a series of paths in your neighbourhood which will enable you to travel in a circle back to your starting point. Identify features marked on your map along your chosen route, such as path junctions, prominent buildings, anything which you think you will easily recognise on the ground and which you can use to pinpoint your position. Using the map, describe the route to yourself as you expect to find it with the landmarks in their correct order. Use the same method as in Chapter 3, Map Reading, paying particular attention to geographical direction and to your "left", "right" and "straight on". If it will help, write down a brief description of the route. Fold your map so that the appropriate area is on view in your map case and then walk your route! Before you move from your starting point make absolutely sure that you have located your starting point on the map with certainty. Then set your map to ensure that you are following the right path and make a habit of setting the map whenever you make a major change of direction or come to another path. Each time you come to one of your selected landmarks, pinpoint your position by checking it against the map. Continue to track or follow your progress across the ground on the map by means of the landmarks on your route. How does the forecast or description you made from the map compare with the reality of your route? Did you recognise the landmarks which you selected or could you have chosen more appropriate ones? Select other routes and keep on repeating the process until it becomes a habit and your forecasts match up with what you encounter on the ground. This technique can be practised anywhere, in the city using street maps, in country lanes or forest paths. Make it easy for yourself at first and then as your confidence grows gradually increase the difficulty of the routes. You do not have to confine yourself to walking, the same method can be used while travelling on a bus, train, or a passenger in a car. Take your 1:50000 Landranger map as your speed of travel will be greater, and try and find a seat at the front of a bus, preferably a double-decker, and then track your position and route on the map. Features will come at you much more quickly than when you were walking and, at first, you may have difficulty adjusting to the speed of travel, but after a little while you will not only be able to track your position but you will be able to anticipate landmarks and what lies ahead with ease. You can follow the same procedure in a car or train. If you have the opportunity to use a train take your map with you as it provides excellent practice. You will, in all probability, be travelling much more quickly and will not have the advantage of being able to look forward; this will sharpen up your map reading and force you to use more distant landmarks from your route. Form the habit of taking a map with you whenever you go out and practising this skill for it forms, along with the ability to set the map, the basis of route finding.

*"Form the habit of taking a map with you wherever you go"*.

## Time and Distance

In the section on map reading we related distance to scale; the time has arrived to carry this relationship further and relate distance to time. Ever since the beginnings of history the length of journeys has been measured in terms of time—"a three day journey", "a day's march". The practice is just as common today. If you ask a passer-by in the city how far away the Post Office is, the most likely answer will be— "Just a five minute walk!" The passer-by in all probability will not have the slightest idea how many yards or metres it is to the Post Office but will be able to visualize the route and express it in a way which you will understand. To express the length of a journey in terms of time is generally more useful and has more meaning than expressing it in units of distance. We do this all the time when we travel by road, rail or air; and we can always add the number of hours the journey takes to the time of departure and form some estimate of our time of arrival at the other end. For the overwhelming majority of travellers over the ages, time has been their only way of expressing distance.

When you plan your next walk, in addition to identifying the route, landmarks and path junctions which will enable you to pinpoint your positions, measure the distance between those junctions where you change direction or take another path. A normal walking pace along roads or footpaths might be around 5 kilometres (3 miles) per hour or roughly 10 or 12 minutes to walk a kilometre. Allow a minute, or just over, for every 100 metres between the junctions and make a note of the distance and the time allowed. Repeat this for the whole of the route. When you start to walk the route make a note of the time or start your stop watch if you have one. Walk at your normal pace, rhythmically and purposefully but do not try to hurry. No matter how far you have to walk you should always have enough breath left to talk normally to a companion! As you pass each landmark pinpoint your position on the map but do not stop or hesitate until you reach the junction to which you measured the distance and estimated the time. Stop and make a note of the time. Set your map, check that you will be heading in the correct direction for the next part of your walk and identify the landmarks to pinpoint your position. Note the time again and then complete the next section of your journey. Keep on repeating the procedure until you reach your destination. After you have completed the journey compare the actual time it took to walk each section with your estimated time. Work out the average time that it takes you to walk a kilometre, 500 metres, 250 metres and 100 metres. Fig. 4.7 and 4.8.

**FIG. 4.7** Time and distance

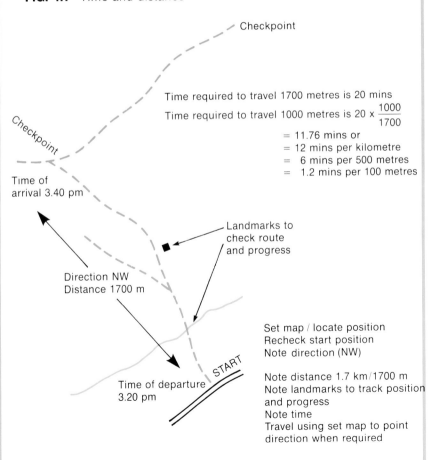

Checkpoint

Time required to travel 1700 metres is 20 mins

Time required to travel 1000 metres is $20 \times \dfrac{1000}{1700}$

$= 11.76$ mins or
$= 12$ mins per kilometre
$= 6$ mins per 500 metres
$= 1.2$ mins per 100 metres

Checkpoint

Time of arrival 3.40 pm

Landmarks to check route and progress

Direction NW
Distance 1700 m

Set map / locate position
Recheck start position
Note direction (NW)

START

Time of departure 3.20 pm

Note distance 1.7 km/1700 m
Note landmarks to track position and progress
Note time
Travel using set map to point direction when required

Make a note of these times so that you can use them to prepare a better estimate for your next walk. Each section of your walk which you time in this fashion we will call a LEG and the place where we stop to check our time and position, or make a major change in direction, we will refer to as a CHECKPOINT. Repeat the process until you are confident that you know how long it normally takes you to walk a given distance. Once you are able to do this you have another important skill to add to your route finding techniques. If, for example, you were expecting to encounter a very obvious landmark 800 metres along your route and it did not show up after 12 or 15 minutes walking at your normal pace, then it would be time to ask yourself if you are on the right route or what has gone wrong.

You do not need to go into the mountains or wild country to find large areas of woodland or forest accessible to the public. These often contain a multitude of paths or rides which may, or may not, be marked on your map. In the absence of manmade landmarks aiding you to pinpoint your position and select the correct change of direction at a path junction, you may have to rely on your estimation of distance. Fig. 4.8.

This method of measuring distance by relating it to travelling time is just as effective for the cyclist, canoeist, rower, rider or cross-country skier. All that is necessary is to work out, from past experience, the average time it takes to travel a kilometre or a part of a kilometre; or a mile and parts of a mile if you prefer Imperial Measure.

There are, in addition two other ways of measuring distance:

One is by pacing—measuring distance by the length of our strides. It is the most accurate method available to the walker, but it is distracting and tedious. There should be little need of such a method in normal or open country and so we will leave this method for a later chapter where greater demands for precision in our navigation may force us to seek more drastic solutions. The other method is the visual estimation of distance.

**FIG. 4.8**  Time and distance

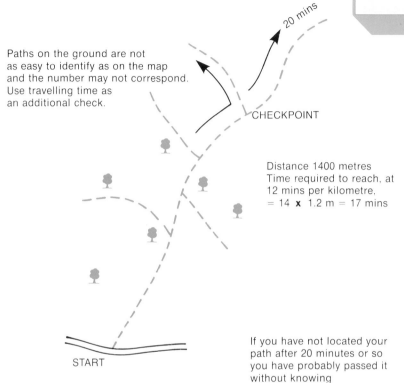

20 mins

Paths on the ground are not
as easy to identify as on the map
and the number may not correspond.
Use travelling time as
an additional check.

CHECKPOINT

Distance 1400 metres
Time required to reach, at
12 mins per kilometre,
= 14 **x** 1.2 m = 17 mins

START

If you have not located your
path after 20 minutes or so
you have probably passed it
without knowing

# Visual Estimation of Distance

This method of measuring distance, as its name implies is the least
precise of the three methods available, and yet it is an extremely
valuable ability for the navigator. Unfortunately, the urban life-style
of the vast majority of the population results in many not knowing
whether a hill is one kilometre away or ten! This frequently makes the
identification or location of features in the landscape difficult or
impossible and often they can see their next objective on the ground
and not know whether it is ten minutes walk away or two hours. You
do not have to become an expert, a little effort will be quickly
rewarded by a vast improvement in your ability to estimate distance
by the eye. Like most other skills it is largely a matter of practice!

*"Estimate the distance of a feature then measure the distance on your map".*

Go back to your vantage point; the top of the hill or tower block. Select a feature in the landscape, but before you identify it by means of setting the map, guess how far away it is. After you have identified it measure the distance from your location using your measuring scale. Now that you know its actual distance have a long and careful look. How big are people, buildings, cars? Try and retain a mental impression of the distance. Repeat the exercise with landmarks nearer and further away and in different directions using your first distance as a "yardstick". Make a habit of guessing or estimating the distance of a feature before you measure the distance on your map, looking up towards hills, from high points looking down or "along the flat". Your viewpoint will influence your appreciation of distance to some extent but this can be ignored for the level of accuracy we require. Fig. 4.9.

78

**FIG. 4.9**   Visual estimation of distance.

- Estimate / guess distance to feature
- Locate feature on map (see 'Identifying a feature')
- Measure distance on map ■ Relate distance to visual impression
- Repeat on features at varying distances and relate to each other

As your ability to estimate distance improves so your ability to locate and identify features on the ground will be speeded up as all the skills reinforce each other.

Before turning your attention to other considerations, find a straight, level stretch of road or path where you can see for a kilometre or more. Using your map, try and select two objects which are visible from each other and are more or less exactly one kilometre apart. This should be as near to where you are based as possible so that you can look along it and walk along it regularly, until you know what a kilometre looks like, and feels like to walk. It will eventually become your own personal measure or "yardstick" which you can then use to measure and visualize other distances.

# The Route Card

The basic skills of this Section should enable you to find your way around normal and open country and you should make every effort to extend your skills and confidence by planning journeys which will take you into country which is unknown to you but still avoiding the mountainous and wild country areas. Though it may not be so important in normal country it is sound practice to form the habit of

**FIG. 4.10** Route Card

The standard route card has been amended
for use in normal or "greenfield" country

| ROUTE CARD (Use one per day) | NAME OF GROUP OR UNIT | | | | | | | | | | | |
|---|---|---|---|---|---|---|---|---|---|---|---|---|
| | ADDRESS | | | | | | | | | | | |
| | TEL. No. | | | | | | | | | | | |
| NAMES OF GROUP MEMBERS | | Setting out time | | | | | | | | | | Supervisor's Name, Location, Tel No. |
| | | Details of route to be followed | Escape to: | | | **D O** | **N O T** | | **U S E** | | | |
| | | Estimated Time of Arrival E.T.A. | | | | | | | | | | |
| | | Total time for leg | | | | | | | | | | |
| | | Time for stops or meals | | | | | | | | | | |
| | | Time allowed for leg | | | | | | | | | | |
| | | Height climbed in m/ft | | | **D O** | | **N O T** | | **U S E** | | | |
| Day of the week | Date | Day of Venture 1st, 2nd etc | Distance in km/miles | | | | | | | | | |
| | | | General Direction or bearing | | | | | | | | | |
| | | PLACE WITH GRID REF | | | | | | | | | | |
| | | START | | | | | | | | | | |
| | | Leg 1 | TO | | | | | | | | | |
| | | 2 | TO | | | | | | | | | |
| | | 3 | TO | | | | | | | | | |
| | | 4 | TO | | | | | | | | | |
| | | 5 | TO | | | | | | | | | |
| | | 6 | TO | | | | | | | | | |
| | | 7 | TO | | | | | | | | | |
| | | 8 | TO | | | | | | | | Totals | |

informing some responsible person of your whereabouts; Youth Organisations and Local Education Authorities usually insist upon it. The most effective method of doing this is by means of a ROUTE CARD. If ever you were missing in mountainous country your safety or well-being may well depend on you being located by means of your route card but they have an equally important function in terms of training. Route cards concentrate the mind, they help you to clarify your intentions and they are an excellent discipline. They bring together the individual skills and weld them into a statement of intent. The experienced mountaineer may well be content for the "route card" to consist of a few names scribbled on the back of an envelope but for the novice, the route card's most important function is to enable past experience to be used for future planning.

Select an area of country on a 1:25000 scale map which is strange to you, yet not too far away. Avoiding roads as much as possible, select a series of footpaths which will enable you to walk in a circle back to your departure point. A total distance of around 8 or 10 kilometres (five or six miles) might be a suitable distance. Divide the route into sections or LEGS on the basis of direction. Whenever there is a major change of direction at a path junction start another leg. Refer to the start of each leg as a checkpoint. Make a copy, or enlarged photocopy, of the route card opposite and then fill in your proposed route.

Fig. 4.10. In the first column enter the location of the checkpoints which divide the route into legs with their Grid References. If the places are identified by a name use the name but if not, use a simple description such as "The junction of path with track", or "The bridge over stream", and then give the Grid Reference. In the second column write the general direction of the next checkpoint from the start, or the previous one, using the nearest of the cardinal and half-cardinal points. After dealing with direction, measure the distances between the checkpoints to the nearest 100 metres and enter the figures in the third column. Filling in these first three columns involves only simple map reading skills but the next involves you making a judgement based on personal experience. Knowing the distance between the two checkpoints, estimate how long it will take you to travel between the two places from your previous experiments in finding out how long it takes you to travel a kilometre or a part of one. At each checkpoint allow yourself a five or ten minute break to note times, set the map and compare map and country, and memorize the features which will enable you to pinpoint your position as you make your way along the next leg. If the checkpoint overlooks the surrounding country so much the better, as you will have an opportunity to practise locating and identifying features. By adding this allowance to the time it takes to walk the leg and then to your starting time you will be able to calculate your time of arrival at the various checkpoints and at your destination. This time is known as the ESTIMATED TIME of ARRIVAL or ETA and it is central to effective planning. The next column is large enough to allow you to describe the method of route finding you are using or the features you are following. "Follow road to junction with footpath". "Follow S. bank of stream". Such a route card would provide a responsible person with a clear understanding of your route, but, of equal importance, it has concentrated your thinking and you have produced a clear statement of your intentions. It is surprising how many lose their way because they only have a vague idea of where they are going.

The specimen route card Fig. 4.10 is similar to the one for mountainous country but with two omissions—there is no provision for the extra time needed for travelling up hill, and there is no space for escape routes or alternative routes to use for bad weather. Escape and alternative routes for bad weather are generally inappropriate for normal and open country. There is no provision for allowing for height climbed for two reasons:

First, although hills and steep climbs are frequent occurrences in normal and open country, they are usually not so high or so prolonged, and they do not dominate movement to the same extent as they do in mountainous country. Secondly, it just introduces another complication, which is usually unnecessary, to your route planning, a complication which is better delayed until the need is greater.

Prepare a route card for a locality which is strange to you but still in "greenfield" country. Then travel to the starting point and follow the route you have planned and see how well your forecast relates to the reality of the journey.

*"Route cards concentrate the mind".*

## Following a Planned Route

Locating your position on the map and setting the map is rarely easier than at the start of your journey. If you are unable to do this at your point of departure, the car park or the bus stop or the front door of the Youth Hostel, then you may well join Robert Louis Stevenson in believing that "to travel hopefully is a better thing than to arrive, and the true success is the labour."

Locate your position on the map and set the map, or vice versa. Recheck your position to make certain. Note the landmarks or features which will enable you to pinpoint your position as far as your first checkpoint. Note any feature at, or near, the checkpoint where you change direction which will help to distinguish it from other paths: "the first road on the left after the Post Office", "the path junction at the stream", even "the track BEFORE the wood" is helpful for at least if you reach the wood you will know that you have travelled too far and missed the turn. Try and memorize details for the first leg of your journey. Note the direction in which you are going to travel, East or North-West etc. Record the time and then depart using your set map to point direction. Track your position on the map by means of the landmarks. Try and avoid stopping but use your map all the time to anticipate the detail and features on the ground. You will find paths and entrances to buildings and farms which are not marked on the 1:25000 scale map, and even less detail on the 1:50000. These may confuse you at first; this is why we have taken the trouble to find some distinguishing feature to identify the place where we change direction and estimated how long it will take to get there. Try to be as observant as possible and make a mental note of the features you pass. Stop when you reach your first checkpoint, note the time and see how it compares with your forecasted time. Look around you and take particular care to look back along the path you have travelled. You should always be able to retrace your steps along a route you have travelled without having to use the map. If you cannot do this your level of observation is too low and you will need to make an effort to improve it. Cavers and potholers make a habit of looking behind them at every passage junction for they have to rely on this procedure to be able to find their way out. Always look back at every major change of direction and take in the scene from the opposite point of view from which you are heading. An occasional glance over the shoulder while travelling is also important. Before setting off on the second leg, carry out the same procedure as you did at the start of your journey:

(**a**) Set your map and locate your position on it.

(**b**) Note the direction in which you are going to travel in terms of the cardinal and half-cardinal points.

(**c**) Estimate the time required to reach the next checkpoint.

(**d**) Identify the landmarks which will enable you to pinpoint your position and memorize them as far as your next checkpoint.

(**e**) Recórd the time and then set off, using your set map where necessary to point direction.

(**f**) Ensure that you are on the correct path by using the landmarks to pinpoint your position and track your progress. Just keep on repeating the process until you reach your destination. This is the basis of all route finding on paths.

The little extra effort required to keep track of your position is well worth while for it is easier to track your position than to sort yourself out if you get lost. Do not, however, let the thought of getting lost inhibit your activity—better to get lost in ordinary country than in the mountains. Being lost is a learning situation; how you tackle the situation is the vital consideration.

Eventually, all the skills and the procedure which at first seems so tedious will blend together to form a habit, and you will find yourself carrying them out quickly and without thinking about them. When you find that you are carrying out the routine without having to think about it, you will know that you have mastered the essential techniques of route finding in ordinary country.

Route planning and following a planned route is the same whether you travel by cycle, canoe, boat or on a horse. Your path may become a river or you may be restricted to roads and bridleways but the

*"Tracking a planned route is the same whether you travel by water or on land".*

procedure is the same; you track your progress by features or landmarks. Your speed of travel may well be different but it is established in exactly the same way by noting how long it takes to cover a given distance. On water, currents may affect your speed of travel according to direction and the wind may also have a considerable influence on journey time. Travelling by motor vehicle involves a similar technique but usually we have road signs to help us. Motor travel in the outback, or where there are no road signs, may well require a high standard of map reading and a procedure similar to that used when travelling on foot, but at least we have the benefit of a speedometer to tell us our speed of travel and, more importantly, an odometer to measure the distance we have travelled.

## SUMMARY

Route finding is based on the ability to set the map and to be able to locate our position on the map. Sometimes we find our position and then set the map, while at other times setting the map may come first and assist in locating our position on the map. With practice it is usually possible to carry out the two processes simultaneously. We need to condition ourselves to look at the set map from any angle.

Once we are able to set the map we can use the set map to:

■ Point our direction of travel or identify the path to take.

■ Give direction in terms of the cardinal and half cardinal points.

■ Locate features shown on the map in the country (map to country).

■ Identify features in the country which are marked on the map (country to map).

It is helpful to travel to some vantage point where it is possible to have a panoramic view of the landscape and to be able to estimate distance visually.

Route finding in normal, open or "greenfield" country is all about selecting and stringing together roads, tracks and paths which will connect departure point with destination and then identifying landmarks along the route which will:

■ Ensure that we are following the right path.

■ Enable us to track progress along the route so that we are able to pinpoint our position on the map.

It is important that we note journey times so that we can work out how fast we travel, so that past experience can be used for future planning. A route card is a most effective way of assisting this process.

Journeys should be divided into sections or legs with an easily identifiable checkpoint at the end of each leg. Before leaving a departure or checkpoint a procedure should be followed:

■ Set map and double check position.

■ Note direction of travel.

■ Estimate time to cover leg.

■ Identify and memorize landmarks from the map for the leg.

■ Note time and depart using the set map to point the way when needed.

Travel purposefully at a steady pace without stopping. Take an occasional glance backwards and be sufficiently observant of the detail of the route to enable the route to be retraced back to the departure point if this should be necessary.

# PART 3

## MOUNTAIN AND WILD COUNTRY NAVIGATION

The techniques of route finding in mountainous or wild country are the same as those used in the normal or greenfield country of Part 2. By far the greater proportion of all travel will take place on paths, not only in the British Isles and the rest of Europe but many other parts of the world as well. Much of the time will be spent stringing footpaths, tracks and trails together to lead us to our destination. There are, however, additional problems which have to be overcome in this kind of terrain and the whole of Part 3 is concerned with tackling these problems. Some of the more obvious differences between mountain and wilderness country and the normal or ordinary country we live in are:

■ The paths may not be as well defined, or there may be too many.

■ The paths are far less likely to be signposted and there is a lower probability of someone being around from whom we can ask the way.

■ There are fewer man-made landmarks and features with which to pinpoint our position or aid our direction finding and we are compelled to rely more on natural features and the shape of the land or even the steepness of slope.

■ There may be no paths at all leading to our destination and we may have to make our own way across country.

■ Mountain weather may have a profound influence on conditions under-foot and on our speed of travel. Higher altitudes increase the probability of having to navigate in hill fog or cloud, or even blizzard conditions.

Remoteness brings its own problems. During the summer months at the weekend, in the British Isles you may have to queue on certain ridges to reach the summit of a number of our better known peaks; while during the week or a few miles away you may be very remote and dependent on your own resources. The consequences of misadventure or inadequate navigation may be much more serious. One of the most frequent causes of mountain rescue teams being called out is walkers losing themselves through inadequate navigation.

Relief has a much more dominant role in the mountains than in lower and flatter terrain. Our speed of travel is affected by both climbing and descent. Climbing uphill limits the distance we can travel, not only because it requires more time but because it is more exhausting. The very steepness of some terrain creates "no-go areas" for the walker and backpacker. Skill and experience are required in reading the map to enable us to differentiate in our planning between those areas which are within our capabilities and those areas where it may be unwise for us to venture.

Just as the skills of Part 2 could only be acquired out-of-doors, so we will need to spend many hours developing the relevant skills of mountain and wild country navigation. For many this will entail travelling, though it will not necessarily involve travelling to a national park or some well known mountain area to start with. Obviously, you cannot learn to navigate in the mountains or wild country without being in that type of terrain, but experience must be built up gradually and progressively and your nearest area of hilly country will be the best place to start this developmental process. Over the course of time you will need to travel to different and more demanding country. Your equipment will have to be able to stand the additional demands which may be placed upon it and a daysack with the appropriate emergency equipment should always be carried. It is of even greater importance that your standards of hill or mountaincraft are always equal to your navigational skills. The development of your navigation and your general mountaincraft must progress together, hand in hand, and be mutually supportive.

Learning to navigate by yourself speeds the process up considerably, but personal safety or the desire for companionship may increase this number. The Duke of Edinburgh's Award and many Youth Organisations insist on a minimum of three in normal or open country and a minimum of four for wild country. The size of a party learning to navigate should be kept to the minimum. You may have to take it in turns at leading and it is essential that the navigator is out in front. All members of the party should have their own maps and equipment

and each member should track the route and carry out the basic techniques. Learning to navigate on a shared map is at best frustrating and, at worst, a waste of time.

You will need to add to your collection of two maps. It is just as important to use a 1:25000 scale map at this stage of your development as it was in learning the basics in normal country, so if there is a hilly area within easy travelling distance of where you are based which is covered by an Outdoor Leisure map, so much the better.

## SUMMARY
Navigation in mountain or wilderness country is largely concerned with following tracks, trails and paths and is based on the same techniques as route finding in normal country, except that there are fewer man-made landmarks to assist in pinpointing position. It is necessary to rely more on the shape of land itself and its representation by contours on the map. Where there are no paths it is usual to use line features such as valleys, ridges or spurs to provide a route or give direction.

So far the only directions we have considered have been the eight major ones which are obviously on the horizontal plane but there are two more which we may be less inclined to consider as directions yet they have an important influence on our navigation—UP and DOWN. The desire to climb or walk up to the summit of a mountain may be the most important reason for being in the mountains in the first place, while at other times the downward direction may follow the successful achievement of the climber's goal, relief from the full force of the elements to the comparative shelter of lower ground, or an escape from hill fog to the better visibility below the cloud base. Up and down are directions which have an additional importance; they are directions which are readily perceived by the eye and there is also a kinaesthetic or body awareness which is absent in the usual geographic directions. We feel the extra demands placed on our body when we travel uphill, we feel in our legs when we travel downwards. When visibility is severely limited up and down may be the only directions which we can perceive and, therefore, they must have an additional navigational significance.

**FIG. 6.1** Few people get lost on the way up

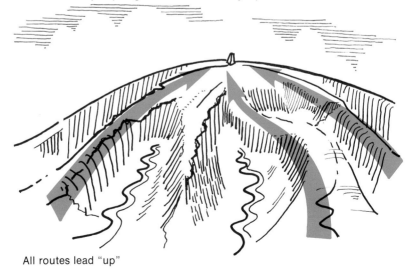

All routes lead "up"

## Up

If the summit of a hill or mountain is our objective then as long as we travel in an upward direction we will eventually reach our objective. In other words the upward direction, so easily appreciated by eye and body, is a most effective route finding aid. It is this factor which accounts for the fact that very few people get lost on their way up to the summit. Fig. 6.1.

## Down

When you are at the summit all directions are "down" but only one way will take you to your destination. This may be compared to someone standing on the North polar icecap; all directions are South but if you move in the direction you are facing you may finish up in Siberia while if you do an about turn you may end up in Canada. When descending we no longer have the strong directional aid which we had during our ascent. This, coupled with the relaxation following the achievement of reaching the top, often takes us off guard which accounts for many getting lost on the way down and often finishing on the wrong side of the mountain and many miles from their intended destination. Fig. 6.2.

**FIG. 6.2** "Down"

Only one route down may lead to your intended destination

## Water

In nature water always seeks to flow directly downhill and so flowing water is an important indicator of up and down and of direction; it acts as a guide or handrail which can lead to less severe weather or habitation. On the map flowing water always crosses the contours at right angles unless it is in an artificial water course. Artificial water courses cross contours at all angles; dykes and ditches concerned with drainage tend to be at greater angles to the contours than canals or leats which tend to follow the contours. A leat is an open watercourse which leads water to a reservoir, dam or mill. Ditches and dykes can usually be identified on the map as they tend to be unnaturally straight, while canals and leats, as mentioned previously generally contour around the slopes. In mountainous country water becomes a much more important indicator of direction and we rely on the mountain streams, the gills, the burns and the becks to a much greater extent in our route finding.

*"A gradient of 1 : 4 is usually about the maximum for motor traffic".*

## Slope Direction

Streams cross contours at right angles and using a set map we can always get direction from streams so we are always able to find the direction of the slope upon which we are travelling. Before the introduction of contours, relief was frequently shown by means of hachures—a line shaped like an elongated arrow-head with the thick end always at the top of the slope and pointing directly down the slope. Fig. 6.3. Hachures are not now used to show relief but we still have an indication of their use in cuttings, embankments, hollows, depressions and mounds. Though we no longer have hachures to orient the slopes for us a line drawn on the map at right angles to the contours will give the direction of the slope and we can set our map from this and at least we should know which side of the hill or mountain we are on. Fig. 6.4.

**FIG. 6.3**   1857 Ordnance Survey Map

*"Hachures indicated slope direction".*   © *Crown copyright*

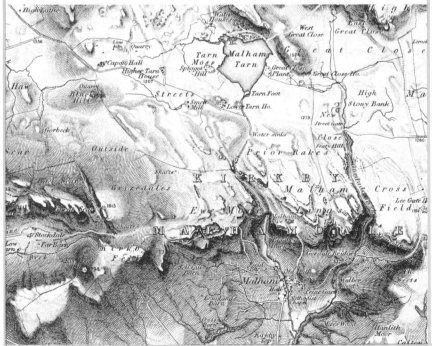

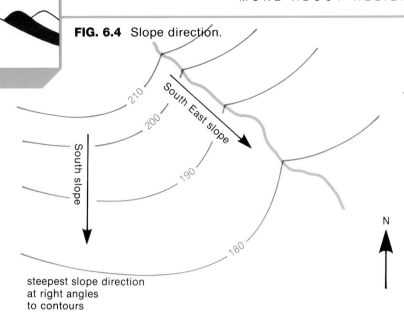

**FIG. 6.4** Slope direction.

steepest slope direction
at right angles
to contours

## Gradient

The steepness of a slope may be expressed in three ways:

(**a**) As the angle the slope makes with the horizontal, eg a slope of 4 degrees.

(**b**) As a ratio, eg 1:4 or 1 in 4.

(**c**) As a percentage, eg a gradient of 25%.

Expressing slope as an angle has little meaning for the ordinary traveller or walker, though it may have more meaning for the climber who has to cope with more severe slopes.

The use of a ratio, the tan, is much more widespread, being the traditional method used by civil engineers and surveyors and we are all familiar with the road signs, 1:10 (one in ten), 1:4 (one in four). A gradient of 1:4 means that in a horizontal distance of 4 units the ground rises 1 unit or it rises 1 metre over a horizontal distance of 4 metres. We are familiar with this method of expression from the road signs on hills. Main roads with a gradient of 1:10 or 1:8 usually attract a warning sign, while a gradient of 1:4 is usually about the maximum for motor traffic, though all who live in the more hilly areas will probably know of the odd hill which is steeper.

Expressing gradient as a percentage is becoming much more frequent and the old road signs are gradually being replaced with their continental equivalents. A 15% slope is one where the ground rises 15 metres in a horizontal distance of 100 metres. So the old road signs indicating 1 in 4 will be replaced with ones showing 25%. Since the metrication of the Ordnance Survey maps this is obviously the most convenient method of expressing gradient for us to use. Fig. 6.5.

The representation of steep slopes on the map can pack the contours so closely together that some have to be omitted, usually the "thin" or intermediate contours, between every fifth thick one. This is especially necessary on the 1:50000 *Landranger* maps where it is not unusual to find lengths of one, two, three or all the intermediate contours deleted. In these areas you will have to rely on the thick contours which are rarely deleted and the magnifying lens on your compass baseplate to extract the full detail of the slope from your map. The deletion of intermediate contours may serve as an early warning that you are leaving the realm of the walker and moving into the domain of the scrambler. For further detail see Appendix 1, where the "Contour Counter" on the measuring scale should be of assistance.

Being able to work out the steepness of a slope from the map is of little value until it can be translated by personal experience into visual impressions or into terms of physical effort. You will need to know the

**FIG. 6.5** Gradients

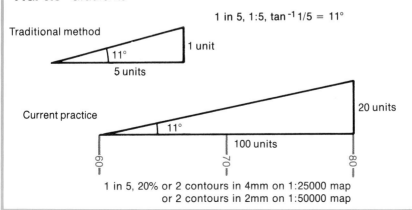

*"When the gradient becomes too steep it is usual to zig-zag".*

steepest slope up which you can walk directly. When the gradient becomes too steep it is usual to decrease the angle of attack by zig-zagging so as to be able to maintain a walking rhythm. You will need to find all this out for yourself but the footpaths and tracks in hilly or mountainous country will help you. By a process of natural selection the paths which have stood the test of time, which may be measured in centuries, are well suited to the walker. Miners, shepherds, drovers and country dwellers balanced the need to keep the distance between two points to the minimum and yet be able to maintain a steady pace and rhythm. They were very concerned with the conservation of energy.

## Slopes

The types of slopes we encounter and their shape may have less impact upon us than their gradient. They do however have a part to play in our route finding. The chances are that, unless we are on an alluvial plain or some other depositional area, practically all our movement

102

takes place on slopes of one sort or another. The type of slope may well determine how much of our route we can see and may even help us to find out where we are.

There are three types of slope:

■ Concave.　■ Convex.　■ Straight or uniform.

(**a**) When we look up a concave slope we see that it gradually increases in steepness and no matter how near or far we are from it we can see the whole of it. Concave slopes usually form the foot of a hill. The contours representing a concave slope gradually come closer together in an uphill direction. Fig. 6.6.

**FIG. 6.6**  Concave slope

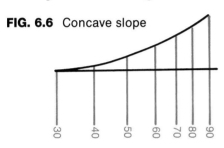

Facing up hill the contours come closer together

All the slope is visible

Usually found at the foot of a hill

(**b**)  Looking uphill, convex slopes decrease in gradient becoming less steep. When we are on a convex slope our visibility up and down is usually severely limited. When moving upwards we are often faced with "false" summits which can be very discouraging to the novice. When travelling downhill the terrain below is again hidden from view and gradually increases in steepness; there is always the danger that it may culminate in a rock face or precipice. Convex slopes usually form the high ground. Facing uphill, the spacing between contours on the map gradually increases. Fig. 6.7.

**FIG. 6.7**  Convex slope

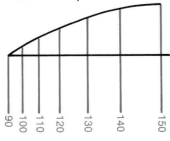

Facing up hill the contours become further apart

Much of the slope is not visible

Usually forms a higher slope

103

(**c**) Straight, uniform or rectilinear slopes are slopes with a constant gradient or angle. Contours are evenly spaced. They do not aid nor impair visibility and are frequently found sandwiched between a convex slope above and a concave slope below. Cliffs may also be straight slopes as are scree slopes which have an angle of roughly 36°.

In a mature landscape, such as the British Isles the concave, straight and convex slopes usually blend together to give a characteristic flattened "S" shaped outline to our hills. Fig. 6.8.

**FIG. 6.8** "S" shape slope

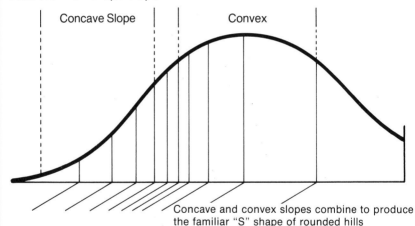

Concave and convex slopes combine to produce the familiar "S" shape of rounded hills

## Landforms

The shape of the landscape is the result of the interaction between the underlying geology and the erosion taking place on the surface. Though there is an endless variety in the landscape it is possible to identify features such as spurs, hills, ridges and valleys which occur over and over again; these landforms are nature's building blocks. We need to be able to recognize them both on the ground and on the map. They are represented on the map by characteristic patterns of contours which help us to visualize the terrain and they often play a dominant role in our route planning in mountainous country. We looked at the hill, valley, and spur in Part 1. We will now extend this range.

## Re-entrant

A subsidiary or side valley; the area of lower ground between two spurs. The term is frequently applied to an elongated depression which does not justify the use of the word valley, owing more to the contour pattern on the map than its significance as a land form. It is usually necessary to spend a considerable amount of time comparing map and country to appreciate the full significance of all the nicks and indentations which appear on contour lines.

**FIG. 6.9** Re-entrants

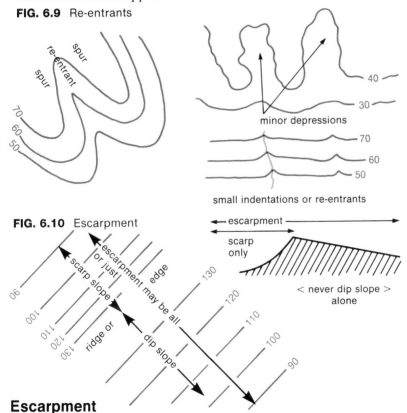

## Escarpment

An escarpment, or cuesta, is a ridge which has a steep, or scarp, slope on one side and a more gentle, or dip, slope on the other. The scarp slope may be a line of cliffs. Sometimes the term escarpment is used for the scarp slope alone but it is never applied to the dip slope alone.

## Ridge

A ridge is formed where two slopes, which are rising upwards towards each other, meet. Ridges may be long narrow spurs or major watersheds. The slopes on either side may be broad and well rounded or very steep. Since there is no English equivalent of arête the word is used for the narrow ridges with steep cliffs between the cirques. Ridges may connect summits together or may lead upwards to summits, as well as being the junction between the scarp and dip slope of an escarpment. Ridge walking is a popular activity for both hill and mountain walkers. See Fig. 6.11.

**FIG. 6.11** Ridge

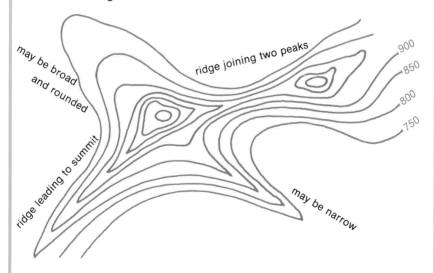

## Edge

The word edge is also used to mark the junction of two slopes. It is easy to distinguish three different uses of the word:

It can be used as a substitute for the French arête, as in Striding Edge on Helvellyn; as the junction of the scarp and dip slopes of an escarpment as in Wenlock Edge in Shropshire; or the outcrop of a line of rock such as Stanage Edge in the Peak District. See Fig. 6.12.

## Arête

An arête is a knife edged ridge usually found between two cirques which frequently has a sharp serrated edge. It may be a small feature or a major watershed. Edge is used as a substitute in England.

**FIG. 6.12** Edge. Can be an arête or escarpment or

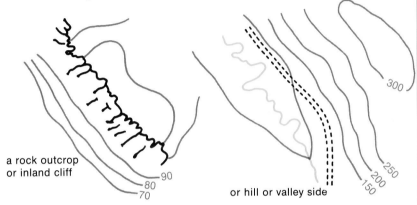

a rock outcrop
or inland cliff

or hill or valley side

**FIG. 6.13** Saddle, Col or Pass

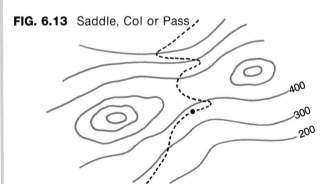

## Saddle, Col or Pass

The lower ground between two hills or mountains, or in a range of mountains, is referred to by one of these three names. Geographers use the French word col. The English words carry a slightly different meaning, pass is generally used for a more significant feature used for communication, while saddle usually indicates a route more likely to be used by travellers on foot. See Fig. 6.13.

107

## Corrie, Cwm or Cirque

Again there is no English equivalent for this feature. Geographers use the French word cirque. A cirque is a deep rounded hollow or basin formed in mountain sides or at the head of a valley. They often have a characteristic armchair shape. They are formed through erosion by snow and ice. The back wall is often a steep cliff but all the walls can sweep up into knife-edged arêtes, as cirques frequently form adjacent to each other. In middle latitudes such as the British Isles cirques often have a preferred orientation which is towards the North-East in the northern hemisphere. Old cirques often have a small lake or tarn in the bottom while active ones are often filled with névé. The contours have a characteristic horse-shoe pattern. See Fig. 6.14.

**FIG. 6.14** Corrie, Cwm or Cirque

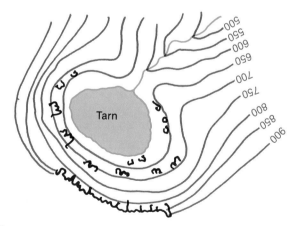

## Truncated Spurs

The spur, a most common landform, has already been considered, but it has a variation which can cause problems for the unwary. A truncated spur is one which has had the end eroded or removed by glacial action. Since spurs are usually well rounded and make an obvious line of descent, a close examination of the contours is advisable in glaciated regions, especially when travelling in bad visibility. See Fig. 6.15.

**FIG. 6.15** Truncated Spur

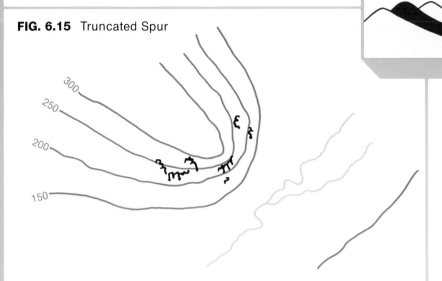

**FIG. 6.16** Hanging Valley

## Hanging Valleys

A hanging valley is a tributary valley which enters the main valley well above the valley floor. The stream of the hanging valley descends in waterfalls or torrents. Hanging valleys are usually, but not always, found in glaciated regions. Where the main valley is U-shaped due to glaciation the streams may descend as spectacular waterfalls, presenting a hazard to the unwary. See Fig. 6.16.

109

## Plateaux

A plateau is an area of flat tableland, the upland equivalent of the plain. Plateaux form many of our moorland areas. Their flatness is relative for they are usually dissected by valleys or dales and they generally have a gentle slope. Both the Pennines and the Cairngorms are dissected plateaux. Because of their height they are more frequently covered in cloud and the lack of outstanding features can make navigation difficult. See Fig. 6.17.

**FIG. 6.17** Plateau

May be tilted with dip slope.
May be disected by streams or rivers.

*"Arête"*.

*"Ridge"*.

111

*TOP: "Saddle".     BELOW: "Cwm/Corrie or Cirque".*

*TOP: "Plateau".     BELOW: "Truncated Spur".*

113

All the features previously described have significance for those who go into the hills and mountains or wild country. They may be the reason for your going there in the first place. Some of them may make travel difficult or even prevent further progress. Some may assist or hinder your route finding. They may help you to locate your position or, by their very number and similarity, cause confusion. These are the most common landforms which you will encounter and they have an important role in determining where you go, and in the absence of man-made features and landmarks you are much more dependent on the shape of the land to assist in your navigation.

The time has come for you to go out and find the features for yourself but it is better to acquire your experience in progressive stages. Select the nearest hilly area to your base, preferably where there is an escarpment or some stiff uphill walking. Plan your route as you have done previously but make the purpose of your walk to study gradient and relief. Using your pencil, divide the route on your map into sections of more or less equal gradient and mark the concave, convex and any straight slopes. Note how many contours per centimetre there are. When you reach your departure point look uphill and see if you can determine the height of the skyline with the aid of the map. Subtract the height of your viewpoint and try and retain a visual impression of what so many metres of height looks like. Set off on your route and note the time taken to cover the various sections. In addition to a visual impression of gradient, try and develop a feeling for the gradient so that when you encounter a slope with the same number of contours per centimetre you will not only be able to visualize it but also have an understanding of the physical effort involved in climbing it. See how the different types of slope affect visibility. When you get to the top set your map and compare the landscape with its representation by means of contours on the map, placing the emphasis on developing an awareness of height, gradients and landforms. By repeating this process a few times and making a conscious effort you will be able to develop a better understanding of relief than many walkers do unconsciously in years. Obviously all the landforms considered in this chapter are not going to be found in one place and

some will only be found in more demanding terrain which may require much more in the way of competence and commitment; before going in search of the corries and arêtes it would be prudent to be able to consider direction and route planning in more detail and the use of the compass.

## Other Methods of Showing Relief

Over the centuries cartographers have found different solutions to the problem of showing height, the third dimension, on a two dimensional piece of paper. So far we have confined our attention to contours. The use of contours for depicting relief is certainly the most widespread and the most useful for the majority of serious map users including those who use maps for route finding. The concept of using contours to show relief is older than many think, it being suggested by a Scotsman in the early eighteenth century, yet the use of contours alone has been a comparatively recent introduction to our maps because contours do not give a strong visual impression of relief except to the experienced eye. In addition to contours, relief can be shown on maps by means of: Hachures; Spot heights; Layer tinting; Hill shading.

*"Hill shading gives a strong visual impression of relief".*　　　　　© *Crown copyright*

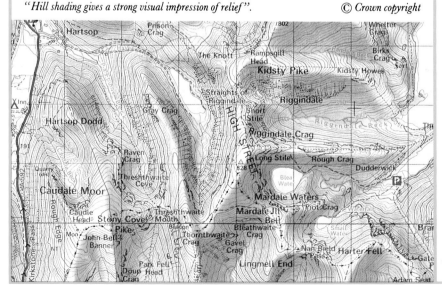

115

## Hachures

Hachures are not used for depicting relief on either the Landranger or the Pathfinder maps so this method can be omitted.

## Spot Heights

The heights of certain places on the map are shown by Spot Heights. The height of hills or the summits of mountains often have their altitudes given in figures. The figures indicate the height in metres above mean sea level at the location of the spot. On older maps and the *One Inch Tourist Maps* the height may be measured in feet. The majority of Spot Heights are to be found along roads and tracks. Where the height has been determined by ground survey the symbol is a small black spot with the height in figures alongside. On the 1:25000 *Pathfinder* and *Outdoor Leisure Maps* in addition to the black Spot Heights there are additional ones, indicated by an orange spot and orange figures, which have been determined by aerial survey.

There are two kinds of Spot Heights where the height has been established with a special precision: Triangulation Points and Bench Marks. Triangulation Stations, frequently referred to as Trig Points are to be found on the tops of hills, mountains or prominent ground. They are marked by the stone or concrete pillars so familiar to hill walkers. Where the height of the ground has been established by levelling the exact spot is marked by a bench mark which is a horizontal bar chiselled into a building or wall or a brass stud; both have a broad arrow underneath.

When you are passing a place which has a Spot Height which has been determined by land surveying, indicated by a black spot, stop and look round, for you may be able to find the bench mark.

By using Spot Heights in conjunction with contours time can be saved; it is frequently possible to find the height of a place without having to trace the contours halfway round the map. In Fig. 6.18; if we wish to find the height of the Quarry we see that there is a Spot Height 127 on the road leading to the quarry. We know that the next contour above must be 130 metres; by counting the contours we find that the altitude of the Quarry is 170 metres. Find from the map the places in your

vicinity which have Spot Heights. Practise finding the heights of places on both your 1:25000 and 1:50000 scale maps using Spot Heights in conjunction with contours.

**FIG. 6.18** Spot Heights

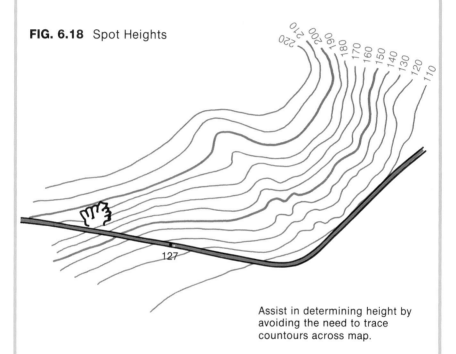

Assist in determining height by avoiding the need to trace countours across map.

## Layer Tinting

This method of showing relief is based on contours. Land on the map between certain contours is tinted in shades, usually of green, yellow, brown, purple or blue. This gives a much stronger visual impression of relief than can be obtained from contours alone. All readers will be familiar with this method from its widespread use in school maps, road maps and atlases. If the colours are too strong detail is obscured and the maps look heavy and oppressive.

117

## Hill Shading

On some maps the slopes facing South East are shaded to form the impression that light is coming from the North-Westerly direction. This hill shading, coupled with layer tinting, gives a very powerful impression of relief. The more recent Ordnance Survey Tourist Maps use layer tinting and hill shading most effectively. The tinting and shading is light enough not to obscure detail; the vital information, height and gradient can be derived from the contours, while the shading and colouring enable the ordinary map user to readily discern the shape of the terrain.

SUMMARY

"Up" and "down" are important directions in their own right; in bad visibility they may be the only ones we are able to appreciate. Slope direction is easily determined both visually and on the map, being perpendicular to the contours. Greater attention should be paid to slope direction, especially when descending, as there is a far greater possibility of getting lost on the way down than on the way up.

The gradients, indicated by the spacing of the contours on the map, must be given meaning by practical experience and observation and the effect of convex and concave slopes on visibility understood.

The range of landforms in Chapter 3 has been extended to include those which not only have a considerable influence on speed of travel, but often determine where we can and cannot go unless we have special experience, skills or equipment as they may present hazards in themselves. They are represented by characteristic contour patterns on the map and exert a considerable influence on our route planning.

Spot Heights, when used in conjunction with contours, are of considerable assistance in finding the height of a place and often avoid the need to trace contours a long way across the map.

Hill shading and layer tinting give a strong visual impression of relief.

In Chapter 1 it was stated that mankind had no innate sense of direction but, by establishing sound habits, you should be able to acquire your own sense of direction which may be of considerable help when the going is tough, or at least spare you the ignominy of finishing up in the opposite direction to which you intended to travel. Hill-farmers, shepherds and most of the other people of the world who live and work, and many of those who habitually take their recreation, in wild and remote places gain their sense of direction from the land itself; they subconsciously memorize the relative positions of the more prominent features of the terrain and then use them as directional aids. By orienting the landscape, the landscape can in turn orient you—by feeding direction into the countryside you can, when the need arises, obtain direction from it. Many hill-walkers and ramblers rely almost entirely on this for their route finding just as travellers have done over the centuries. Nearly all landscapes have a "grain" or pattern, especially hilly or mountainous areas, which can impart a strong directional influence.

### Take a simple instance as in Fig. 7.1.

You are at Point A, in a wide vale. On your right you have a range of hills; they could be the Hambleton Hills, the Quantocks or any one of hundreds of others, even the South Downs, because the geographical direction is not important. You travel in the direction of the arrow. As long as you maintain that direction the hills or escarpment will remain on your right. If they cease to be on your right hand side then you have changed your direction of travel! If you find that you are travelling directly towards them, then your direction of travel is now at right angles to your original course. If you wished to find your way back to your starting place then all that is necessary is to turn until the range of hills is on your left hand side. Direction of travel can be related very easily and effectively to the locality we are in. Valleys, ridges, escarpments, a range of hills (and it does not matter how distant they are) coast-lines, rivers and lakes, provided they are readily visible, all make excellent local direction reference features.

**FIG. 7.1** Direction from a line of hills.

We do not have to confine ourselves to linear features to obtain direction. In hilly or mountainous country the summits and peaks, often with their distinctive shape and outline, form excellent local directional reference points. By relating movement to their relative positions it is possible not only to determine our direction of travel, but to have also a very good idea of our location.

In wild country we have to rely mainly on natural features for our direction, but in England, Wales and some parts of Scotland even the upland areas have not escaped the intrusion of the television mast. They are particularly prominent and are usually visible over many miles and, though we may disapprove of their presence, they make excellent directional reference points. Because they are frequently visible from so far away it is possible to journey for a considerable period of time, or travel round a whole tract of country, and yet still utilize the same point of reference as a directional marker. A not unsimilar form of intrusion has also occurred over the last twenty years or so in the same upland areas; at night the glow of light from our towns and cities has destroyed the black velvety sky with its

*"Even upland areas have not escaped the intrusion of the television mast"*.

thousands of stars. This is particularly marked in the Pennines, but even as far North as Inverness it is frequently possible to navigate at night without the use of the compass and just rely on the orange glow of town and city street lighting to indicate direction. When it is cloudy the glow reflected off the cloud base, just like ice blink in polar latitudes, is even more noticeable. We may regret the loss of our night sky and all but the brighter stars, but make the most of these directional markers. In and around our great conurbations there is just so much light at night that it ceases to act as a directional aid but in many upland areas it can considerably assist travel at night. It is important that the town or city from which the light is coming is either correctly identified, or it is only used as a direction marker.

Whether by day or night, in normal visibility, it is usually possible to find features which will act as local directional markers to which we can relate our direction of travel. Nearly all who would claim to have a good sense of direction have this ability to relate their direction of

travel to the features in their local environment. Though they travel and change direction with ease and confidence they are not equipped with an extra sense—they are just observant and aware of their surroundings with a keen eye for detail. Through experience they will also have acquired some other attributes. In addition to having a good appreciation of distance travelled, they will be very conscious of all the changes of direction they make and tend to store the changes in their memory.

This sense of direction can be acquired by you but, like most things worth having, it will have to be worked for, especially if you wish to speed the process up. In Part 2 we had a procedure to follow before leaving our point of departure or commencing a leg of our journey:

■ Set map and locate position or vice versa.

■ Double check that the starting point is correctly identified.

■ Identify and check direction of route and estimate time for leg.

■ Memorize land or way marks on the first section or leg.

■ Note time and depart using the set map to point direction when necessary.

This procedure, concerned with movement along paths in normal or open country, concentrated attention on the route and the landmarks within its immediate vicinity. In mountainous or wilderness areas it is necessary to take a much more comprehensive view of the landscape in addition to carrying out the usual procedure. On reaching your departure point for your venture, set the map and locate your position in the usual way but, before concentrating on your route, orient the whole of the landscape. It may be necessary sometimes to move to a better viewpoint. Survey the whole of the country into which you are going to move and, using your oriented map, work out the direction of all the principal landforms and features such as valleys, spurs, ridges or the line of the hills or mountains in terms of the cardinal and half-cardinal points. After you have done this look around for prominent and distinctive features around the horizon which will act as direction

123

markers for the locality and make a mental note of their direction. Five or ten minutes spent surveying and familiarizing yourself with the landscape and then feeding direction into it before you set out will be amply repaid during the course of your journey, for you will not only be able to use the countryside to orient yourself when the need arises but, by making a habit of this procedure, very quickly acquire a sense of direction. Whenever you move to an unfamiliar area, or your journey takes you into fresh terrain, repeat the procedure. A good time to carry out this survey and orientation is before commencing each leg of your route when it is beneficial to reward yourself with a ten minute break.

The wild country areas of the British Isles are diminutive compared with the majority of those which exist in other parts of the world, but to many young city dwellers engaged in their first ventures they appear endless and daunting in their vastness, this being especially so in some parts of Scotland. Experience and habituation make the size more manageable in the course of time especially if experience is built up gradually and progressively. This process can be speeded up and the development of your sense of direction assisted if, while you are carrying out your preliminary five or ten minute survey and orientation of the landscape, you do something else as well—frame the area in which you are going to travel. Even wild country is not one endless tract— it is divided into areas by roads, rivers, watersheds, ridges and valleys amongst other things. As you orient the countryside, construct a frame around the area in which you are going to move or work. The boundaries to your frame should, where possible, have two qualities:

**1.** You should be instantly aware if you should stray across them.

**2.** Be visible from as far away as possible.

Roads, rivers, coasts and lakes make excellent boundaries, but well marked tracks and major streams and burns can also be used. Watersheds, summit ridges and escarpments also serve. The frame may well be the perimeter of a wood or forest, a valley bottom, the flank of a mountain or a plateau. Once you have cut the country down

to size it becomes much more manageable and far less daunting. You have now only a patch of country to contend with even though it may be a very extensive patch in some parts of the world. The frame you have constructed around your area of travel, like a picture frame, focuses attention but more importantly it is a reference frame. The direction of your movements, along, across, diagonally, can now be related to the boundaries which compose the frame. Obviously, you may have to construct fresh reference frames as your journey progresses but the process only takes a few minutes and is an essential part of that initial appraisal and comparison of map and country which every prudent traveller makes.

*"Roads, rivers, coasts and lakes make excellent area boundaries".*

## SUMMARY

A sense of direction can be acquired by conscious effort. This sense of direction is nearly always obtained from the landscape itself. Once a landscape has been oriented it can, when required, provide orientation.

Line features, such as valleys, ranges of hills and escarpments, as well as distinctive landmarks such as peaks, all assist in orienting the landscape. Man-made features such as television masts may assist, and at night the light from distant towns or cities may be used as direction markers.

A frame or boundary should be constructed, out of such line features as roads and rivers, around the area in which we are travelling. Movement can be related to this frame; we should be aware if we stray beyond the boundaries and the boundaries can act as collecting features if we should get lost and need something to aim at.

In addition to the usual ritual before leaving a departure or check point mentioned in previous chapters, sufficient time should always be allowed to orient the landscape and construct a boundary around the area in which you are going to travel.

# CHAPTER 8

# USING THE COMPASS

The introduction of the compass into this book has been delayed for as long as possible so that your route finding can be based solely on the use of the map and to provide time for the foundations of a sense of direction to be laid down. The time has now arrived when, if your navigational skills are to be developed further, you will need to go into the mountains or wilderness country. Prudence demands that if there is the possibility of being engulfed in cloud, overtaken by darkness or your map reading is not yet up to the standards required in wild country, you should have the compass to fall back on.

Introducing the compass brings a new factor into your navigation. Instead of direction being externally based, coming either from the country directly or through the medium of the map, you now have a self-centred directional facility. It is possible with the compass to travel in any specified direction without reference to any external landmarks, giving you a navigational potential on a par with, or even in excess of, homing pigeons and migratory animals. On land the compass never gives that same freedom of movement that it gives to the sailor or the pilot of a plane because the land itself usually is a constraint on our movement, frequently determining where we can and cannot go but it is "an ever present help in time of trouble."

The modern protractor type compass has that simplicity which is usually associated with a stroke of genius—that of combining the magnetic compass with a protractor. Before its introduction, to use the prismatic compass you needed, in addition to the compass itself, a protractor, paper, pencil, an extra pair of hands and the ability to do mental arithmetic on a windswept mountainside. The orienteering, or protractor, type compass represents excellent value for money; it is robust and simple to use. In spite of, or may be because of, its simplicity the teaching of the compass in schools and Youth Organizations is often woefully inadequate. Young people quickly develop a superficial skill which enables them to find their way around countryside in which ordinary ramblers would rely entirely on the map if they bothered to use anything at all! Because of their lack of map reading skill they are sometimes reduced to using the compass to determine

whether to turn left or right out of the car park. When they are enveloped in thick hill fog and they have to use their compasses in earnest then the superficial skills fall apart, resulting in a lost and demoralized group afraid to go anywhere. Regrettably the compass has, all too frequently, become a device which enables the incompetent to lose themselves more efficiently. As a result of questioning hundreds of young people over a working lifetime as to why they got lost, or had to be found, when they all had the use of a compass; the answers always indicated one or more of three conditions:

■ Their map reading skills were insufficient to provide a foundation for the use of the compass.

■ Their compass techniques were inadequate for the prevailing conditions.

■ They were so anxious or distressed that they could not navigate adequately or they felt unable to travel.

Many find the total isolation of thick cloud and darkness in the mountains, especially when there is the presence of precipitous slopes, a frightening experience. In the final analysis, using the compass in restricted visibility in wild country is not about technique, it is about mental attitude; having the resolve, the mental toughness to cope with the situation. This mental attitude can only come from the confidence of knowing that both your map reading and compass techniques are of the highest order and that they have been tested by experience. You may well have to make a considerable effort to acquire your compass skills, and it will almost certainly involve some work at night as it is difficult to arrange cloud to order unless you live in one of the higher Pennine towns or villages where you can well spend a considerable part of your life above the cloud base. If you learn your compass skills on a playing field you may well find at the end of the day, when the real call is made, that you have only succeeded in training yourself to find your way round a playing field with a compass!

## The Compass

As suggested in Chapter 2, equip yourself with a protractor type compass with a base at least 10 cm long, damped to enable the magnetic needle to settle quickly—the needle should be contained in a liquid filled capsule. Fig. 8.1. Please yourself whether it is luminous or non-luminous, but it should have a cord so that you can attach it to yourself. Though it is robust, it should be treated with the respect that a highly sensitive instrument deserves. Do not drop it or expose it to excessive heat, keep it away from radiators and glove compartments of vehicles or the capsule may develop a bubble, which depending on its size, may impair the efficiency. Store it away from other compasses, steel and iron objects, electrical appliances and electric circuits.

**FIG. 8.1** The Compass

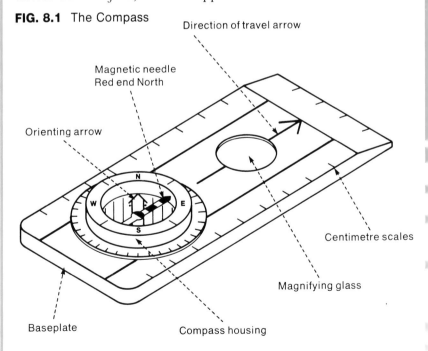

The red, or North seeking, end of the compass needle points to the earth's North magnetic pole, or Magnetic North. This is distinct from the True North, the axis around which the earth rotates. The difference, expressed in degrees, between the True North and Magnetic North is known as the Magnetic Variation. Sometimes the word Declination is used instead of Variation but the traditional British usage is Variation. Magnetic Variation changes from place to place and from year to year and the rate of change is not constant. The difference between Magnetic North and True North is shown in the marginal information on your map.

Deposits of iron-based minerals in the earth's crust can cause local anomalies in the magnetic field which can cause problems in a few localities, but more importantly large iron or steel objects, or objects which contain steel or iron, can have a very strong influence on the compass. It is futile using a compass propped against a motor vehicle or steadied on an iron fencing post. The larger the amount of ferrous metal, the greater and wider the influence on the magnetic needle. Compasses are also strongly affected by the elctro-magnetic fields created by power lines and electric wiring. More insidious is the influence caused by cameras, exposure meters and the ferrous objects we carry with us. I have seen heavy pen-knives attached to the same lanyard as the compass and presumed that in bad visibility the users followed their own pen-knives around the mountains. Take your compass and all the iron or steel objects which you carry around with you on your person or in your pack and find out for yourself what effect they have on your compass as they are brought closer to it. Don't forget to see what effect your watch has! Most people have their watch on their left wrist and hold their compass in their left hand while they rotate the housing with their right hand. See if your torch or headlamp exerts any influence at a normal working distance and don't forget the items which you may only use occasionally, such as your ice axe. After you have tested everything decide on any precautions which you may need to take.

## Keeping Things Simple

### Three Skills

The magnetic compass is a very versatile instrument and there are many techniques associated with its use. In addition to using it to travel on a bearing—getting from A to B in a straight line, its most common use throughout the ages, you can use it to find your position by resection, identify features, locate features shown on your map, amongst other techniques. Some organizations and instructors teach all the major techniques, presumably on the assumption that if you know about the more difficult ones then there is a greater chance of understanding the simple ones, a form of educational overkill. It is my experience that amongst people who only use a compass infrequently, or only in an emergency, this generally leads to confusion, often at a critical or stressful juncture. There are three vital compass techniques which you must master:

■ Travelling on a bearing.

■ Setting the map by compass.

■ Checking the direction of a path.

These are skills which get you out of difficulties and enable you to reach your destination safe and sound. You could spend a lifetime mountain walking and find these three skills sufficient for your needs, and if all mountain walkers were proficient in these techniques there would be fewer demands on the rescue services. If, as your experience increases, you find that you are using the compass frequently and on a regular basis with no mental hang-ups, add the other compass techniques in Chapter 13 in Part 4 to your repertoire.

### The British Isles

As the overwhelming majority of readers will use their compass skills within the confines of the British Isles, it will help to keep techniques, procedures and explanations as simple as possible if, in this chapter, we confine our attention to the use of the compass in the British Isles, where the Magnetic Variation is always to the West of True North,

and will remain so until well into the next century, and, unlike many foreign maps, there are grid lines on the maps we use for navigation. If you intend to use your compass in the Alps, the Himalayas or other places in the world the techniques of this chapter are the same, but you may have to make the adjustments outlined in Chapter 13.

## Measuring Direction

For our map reading needs it is sufficient to express direction in terms of the cardinal and half-cardinal points, but for compass work, where greater accuracy is required, it is necessary to be able to measure direction in degrees. Direction is measured from the North always in a clockwise rotation. The right angle between North and East is divided into 90 degrees; similarly there are another 90 degrees between East and South and so on back to North. Fig. 8.2.

**FIG. 8.2** Measuring direction in degrees

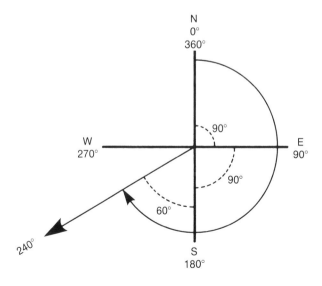

In addition to the True North and Magnetic North mentioned earlier there is a third North—Grid North. Grid North is the northerly direction of the North-South grid lines on a map. While Grid North and True North coincide on the meridian on which the grid is based (2 degrees West) there is a divergence which increases as you move away from the centre of the grid to the East or West. The difference between Grid North and True North is so small that for all practical purposes using the protractor type compass it can be ignored; even on the boundaries of the grid it only amounts to two or three degrees. Directions are measured from the North-South Grid lines and are known as Grid Bearings. Fig. 8.3.

**FIG. 8.3** North

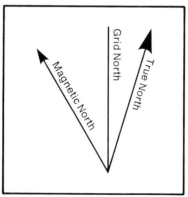

Diagrammatic only

It should always be borne in mind that the protractor type compass has two functions—as a protractor for measuring angles and as a compass for giving direction. When it is used in the hand for sighting it is being used as a compass for giving direction. When it is in contact with the map it is being used as a protractor for measuring angles and it does not matter which way the needle itself is pointing as the needle is ignored at this stage. THE ONLY EXCEPTION IS WHEN THE COMPASS IS BEING USED TO SET THE MAP.

# Travelling on a Bearing

This is the most vital skill, the "life-boat drill" for any traveller in mountainous or wilderness country. It has three steps:

■ Finding the grid bearing from your location to your objective.

■ Converting the grid bearing to a magnetic bearing.

■ Travelling on the magnetic bearing.

Each of the above steps must be practised until they can be carried out automatically, even if your mind is numb with cold or befuddled with anxiety.

**FIG. 8.4** Taking a bearing

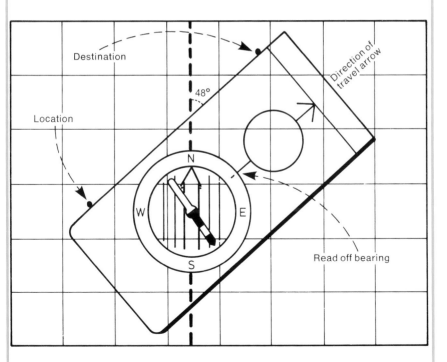

## Finding the Grid Bearing

Place the compass on the map with the top edge of the compass connecting your location with your destination, and with the direction of travel arrow pointing the way you wish to go. Turn the compass housing until the orienting lines on the base are parallel with the North/South grid lines on the map and the "N" on the housing is pointing to the top of the map. The grid bearing can now be read off the scale on the housing opposite the direction of travel arrow. Fig. 8.4. Practise doing this until you can do it quickly and accurately. After dark turn out the lights in the room and, using the torch from your emergency pack, practise finding bearings, resting the map on your knee or the floor until you have solved the light problem and can achieve the same level of accuracy which you could in daylight on a table. The next time you are out in the dark when it is wet and windy, practise again!

*"Woodland is a good place to start".*

*"After dark turn out the lights in the room and, using the torch from your emergency pack, practise finding bearings. The next time you are out in the dark when it is wet and windy practise again!"*

## Converting the Grid Bearing to a Magnetic Bearing

Since the Magnetic Variation in the British Isles is to the West of True North, the variation is always ADDED to the Grid Bearing. There are various ways of remembering this but probably the best way is to reason that, since the country is always larger than the map, the grid bearing should always be made larger when working from the map to country.

For example using a variation of 6 degrees West:

| | |
|---|---|
| Grid bearing | 48° |
| Variation | +6° |
| Magnetic bearing | 54° |

In practice, immediately after you have found the grid bearing, add the variation by turning the housing anti-clockwise for 6 degrees. Always remember to check the variation for the area in which you wish to travel when planning your route.

## Travelling on a Bearing

After the variation has been added, hold the compass horizontally in front of you so that the needle is swinging freely. Then turn yourself around until the red end of the compass needle is pointing to the North on the compass housing and is parallel to the lines in the bottom of the housing. Sight along the direction of travel arrow at some feature in the landscapes; it could be a tree, a clump of grass or a hump on the ground, then travel towards it. You are now travelling towards your objective. Fig. 8.5. When you reach the point you sighted on, stop and repeat the process until you reach your destination. With practice it is possible to become very quick and accurate in taking these sightings. Once you have made your sighting fix your eyes on the spot in question; there is no need to look at the compass again until you get there. In the British Isles it should only be necessary to use this method of navigation very rarely in normal visibility, perhaps in wooded country or particularly featureless areas, but in bad visibility or at night it may become the only effective way of making progress. You must practise for these eventualities. Finding a suitable place for

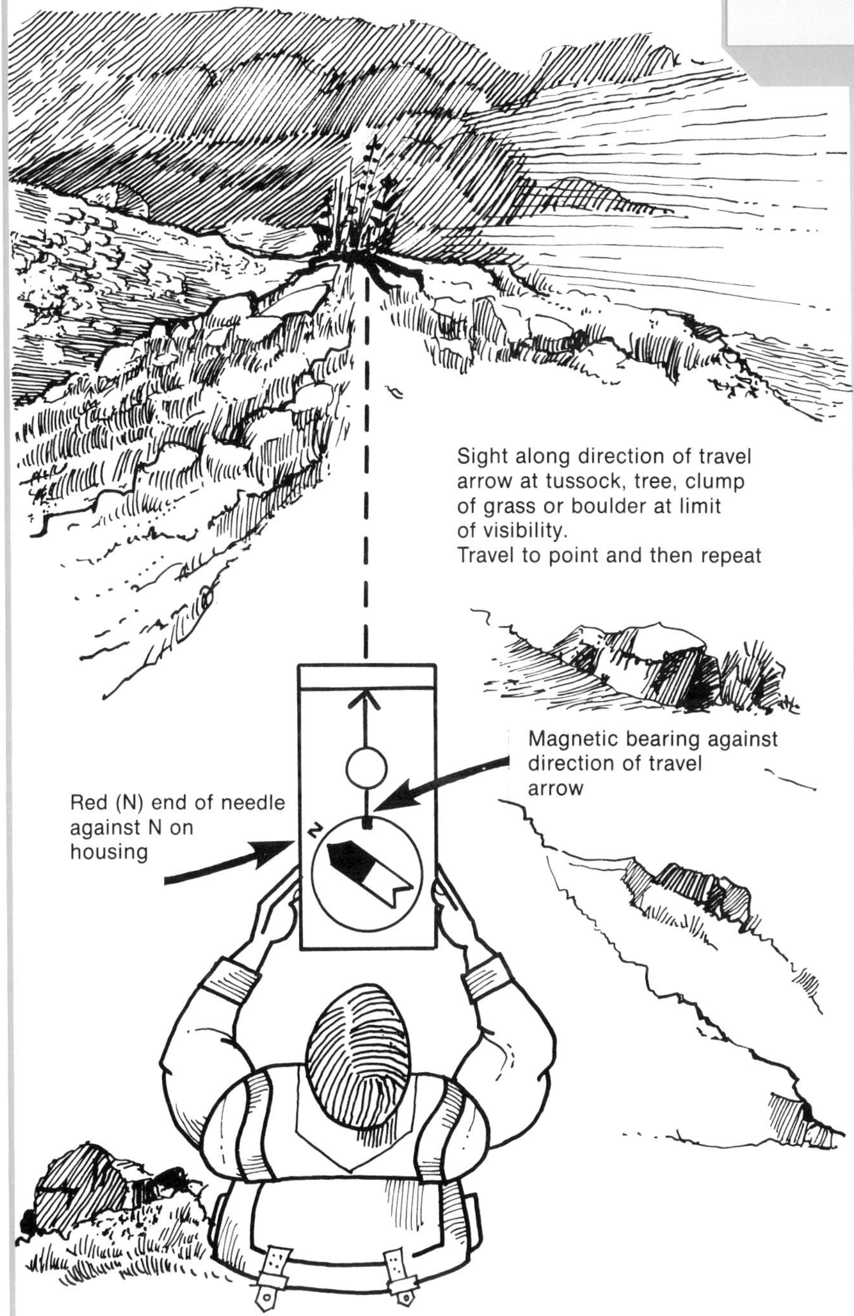

**FIG. 8.5** Travelling on a bearing (Third stage)

Sight along direction of travel
arrow at tussock, tree, clump
of grass or boulder at limit
of visibility.
Travel to point and then repeat

Magnetic bearing against
direction of travel
arrow

Red (N) end of needle
against N on
housing

139

effective practice of this third stage is not easy. Deciduous woodland is a good place to start if you can obtain access to an area in your locality, especially if visibility is restricted so that you need to take sightings every fifty or a hundred metres. Plot a bearing across the wood or a corner of it, from one identifiable point to another so that you can see how accurate you are at hitting your target. Practise until you are accurate at distances between 500 and 1000 metres but remember that it is the number of sightings which you have to make—not the distance travelled which is important.

Though there has been a tremendous increase in the amount of coniferous forest in the upland areas of Britain in recent years, the chances are that when you need to use your compass to get yourself out of a difficult situation it will be on a moor or bare mountain. When compared with continental Europe, the tree line in Britain is very low for a number of climatic reasons such as—high rainfall and leached soils, high winds and a short growing season—not to mention the grazing of sheep. One would be hard pressed to identify woodland above the 550 metre (1800 ft.) contour, possibly in the shelter of some cliff or gill. To gain experience under these conditions you will need to find yourself an area of convex hillside covered in grass, though bracken and heather will do. The convex hillside will force you to make repeated sightings as you travel up or diagonally across. The lack of features on the surface will give you practice in sighting on a particular spot or clump grass; fixing your gaze on it and then travelling towards it.

Having progressed from wood to bare convex hillside the next stage in the progression is to do it in the dark. You may feel that a companion, or companions are necessary for safety's sake, even if they are only within earshot of your whistle. A wood or the same convex hillside are again ideal but, providing there are no lights in the vicinity, any broken, undulating ground or heath may provide realistic conditions, but remember to work out the bearings on the ground using your emergency lighting.

On a ship or a plane, once a compass bearing has been selected all that is required is to keep the bearing opposite the lubber-line to ensure that the craft is on course. We cannot do this. We have to use the protractor compass as a sighting compass and select some mark on the ground or landscape to aim at. If we do not do this and just confine our attention to the compass, and the direction of travel arrow, there is a tendency to "side-slip"—we point ourselves, or head, in the right direction but we drift to one side or the other. This is very likely to happen in strong winds with driving rain or snow, on a slope, or in bad visibility. Fig. 8.6. It is important that the person who is using the compass should be out in front when a group is travelling on a bearing, to avoid being deflected by other members of the party.

**FIG. 8.6** "Side-slipping"

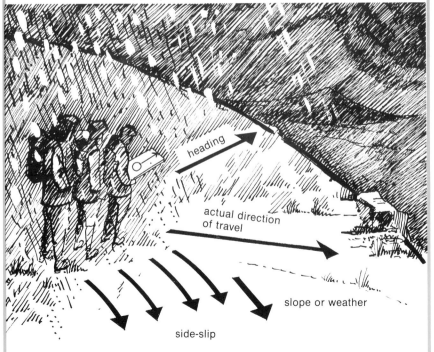

In restricted visibility we aim for a point near to the limit of visibility, but in featureless terrain, where it may be possible to see for many miles, the landmark we sight on may be a considerable distance away. In good visibility, providing we can keep the feature we sighted on in view, it is possible to deviate from the bearing to find an easier path. Fig. 8.7. As a precaution, always make a habit of checking all bearings by relating them to the cardinal and half-cardinal points.

## Tracking Position

Travelling on a compass bearing does not relieve one of the need to carry out that other vital function of route finding—keeping track of position and progress. In restricted visibility, or in featureless terrain, the need is even greater and the maximum use must be made of any clues which will indicate position. In Fig. 8.8, the line of crags at A would indicate if one was off course, while at B, the steepening of the slope would establish position. Similarly, the streams at C1 and C2, would mark progress along the bearing, and their direction should enable any corrections to the course to be made.

**FIG. 8.7** Travelling on a bearing in featureless terrain in good visibility

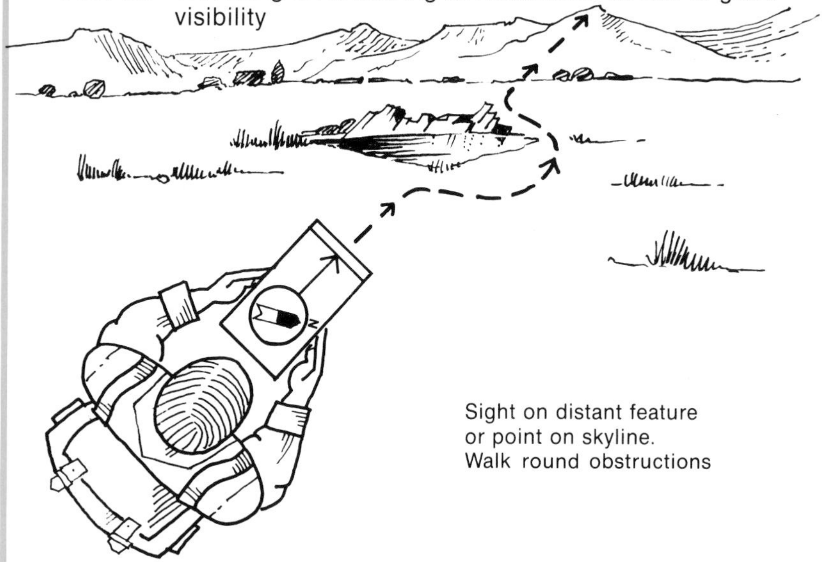

Sight on distant feature
or point on skyline.
Walk round obstructions

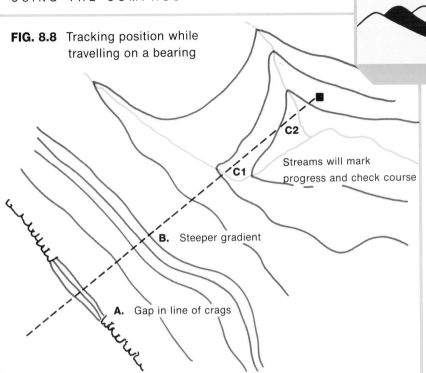

**FIG. 8.8** Tracking position while travelling on a bearing

C2

Streams will mark progress and check course

C1

**B.** Steeper gradient

**A.** Gap in line of crags

# Pacing

Hill walkers find out how far they have travelled from the map. The only other realistic method they have at their disposal is to calculate the distance travelled from the time they have been walking. There is another method—pacing—counting the number of steps and then working out the distance travelled. Over the distances involved in the mountains this method would be extremely tedious, distracting and frequently impossible; the cotton grass moors, peat hags and cloughs of the Pennines immediately spring to mind. Pacing has, however, a long and ancient history, it is regularly used by orienteers and has an important, if limited, role for the hill walker. The unit of distance in Imperial Measure, the mile, is derived from the Latin "mille passus", a thousand double paces of a Roman soldier, although the Roman mile was shorter than the present statute mile, probably of 1618 or 1620 yards. When travelling in restricted visibility on a compass bearing, for example in thick cloud on a mountain summit, it may be essential to travel an exact distance to bring you to the correct path which leads down. This is where pacing comes into its own; when the

143

distances are not excessively long, accuracy is essential and the stakes are fairly high. The hill walker is unlikely to use pacing as a measure of distance except when using the compass to walk on a bearing in restricted visibility; which is why it has been introduced here rather than in an earlier chapter.

The first task is to see how many double paces you need to cover 100 metres. You will need to measure 100 metres with reasonable accuracy. Acquire a ball of thick string or twine and a measuring tape. Fasten a peg to one end of the string and then using the tape, measure out 20 or 25 metres of string, keeping the string fairly taut. Fasten a peg at the end. You now have a measure 20 or 25 metres long. Take your measure to a straight, level footpath, place a marker and then using your length of string, measure out 100 metres (5 lengths if 20 m, 4 if

*"Pacing has an important, if limited, role for the hill walker".*

25 m long). Place another marker. Walking at your usual speed and using a normal stride, count the number of double paces, left foot to left foot or right foot to right foot required to cover the 100 metres. Note the number required. Repeat two or three times and then record the average number of paces required. If you wish to reinforce this experience do the same thing on grass and then see what effect your backpack has. With a little practice pacing can be a very effective method of measuring distance. It can be made even more efficient and reliable if a scale is used, Appendix 1. Practise walking on a bearing but now measure the distance travelled as well!

## Setting the Map by Compass

When the usual methods of setting the map have failed, the country is featureless, or you do not know where you are, the map can be set by using the compass. Just place the compass on the horizontal map and turn the map round until the magnetic needle in the compass is parallel with the North/South grid lines on the map and the red, North seeking end, is pointing towards the top, or North, of the map. There is no need to bother with magnetic variation, the map will not be more than some six or seven degrees out of true in mainland Britain, less than the error brought about by handling the map out of doors.

## Checking the Direction of a Path with the Compass

Usually the direction of a footpath can be checked by using the map alone. With the map set, a pencil laid along the path on the map should point along the path on the ground. But this is not always possible for a variety of reasons. To check the direction of a path, or your route, point the direction of travel arrow along the path (there must be a sufficient length of path visible to give a true indication of where the path is leading). Holding the compass still, turn the housing round until the needle is parallel to the lines in the bottom of the housing and the red end of the needle is opposite the "N". Place the compass on the map with one edge along the presumed path and the direction of travel arrow pointing the way you are going. If you are

following the right path the orienting lines on the bottom of the compass housing will be within five or six degrees of parallel with the North/South grid lines on the map. If the difference is more than 10 or 15 degrees you are most probably on the wrong path. It is a quick and simple check. As in setting the map, no allowance has been made for magnetic variation, but the chances of two paths having a direction within seven, ten or even fifteen degrees of each other are extremely small.

## SUMMARY

The protractor type compass is simple to understand and use. This often leads to a superficial skill which is unable to match up to the demands made by restricted visibility in mountainous or wild country. Considerable effort must be made to achieve realistic training conditions for the compass skills. Woodland, convex hill slopes and darkness should be used to master the skill of sighting quickly and accurately. Until compass skills have been tested by restricted visibility they should always be regarded as being suspect.

All the iron or steel objects carried on the person or in the pack should be tested to see what influence they have on the compass needle.

Practise working out bearings on your map in the dark and using your compass with only your emergency lighting to assist you.

In this chapter only a westerly magnetic variation has been considered to avoid confusion. Magnetic Variation in the British Isles will remain to the West of True North for the rest of this century and into the next. Those who wish to use the compass abroad should refer to Chapter 15. "Using your map and compass abroad".

Where the compass is only used infrequently or in an emergency, it may be wise to limit the skills to three vital ones:

- ■ Travelling on a bearing.
- ■ Setting the map by compass.
- ■ Checking the direction of a path or route.

Route planning, like all other skills, improves with practice, but in no aspect of navigation is there a greater need to use past experience for future planning. The logs and journals of mariners, pilots, navigators and explorers are all testimony to the need to keep some account of a venture to use for future activity. Your route card is more than a method of telling someone where you are going in the mountains so that in the event of misadventure something may be done to help you; it is an effective way of recording your experience for future use.

The first consideration must always be to plan a route which will satisfy the purpose of your journey. It may be to climb a mountain, a few days backpacking or a high level walking holiday in the Alps. Just as the flight plan of an aircraft is limited by its performance, so your route plan must be within your capabilities. An aeroplane has an operational range and an economic cruising speed; similarly there is a limit to the distance you can travel without seriously depleting your reserves of energy and you will have an optimum speed of travel whether you are walking, on a horse or a bike. Just as an aircraft can

*"All land has some use to its proprietor"*.

148

*"High level traverses of well known ridges make a stimulating day out".*

sacrifice range for extra pay-load so you may find it necessary to reduce distance to carry a heavy pack. Routes are not determined by physical stamina alone; experience and skill are of equal importance, the ability to cope with snow and ice, or the scrambling or climbing involved in negotiating a gully, may be vital in determining the route. There should be no need to mention that if you have not got the specialized equipment which these conditions may demand then there is no alternative but to plan a different route. High level traverses of well-known ridges, and the ascent of a series of peaks, which make a stimulating day out for the hill walker with a day-sack, a packet of sandwiches and a few items of emergency equipment, may be quite unsuitable for a backpacker engaged in a venture lasting three or four days. Excessive mileage, an overweight pack and a lot of climbing leads to exhaustion and, in the cold wet climate of the British hills exhaustion and exposure go hand in hand.

## Access

Although journeys often take place in remote areas where, at first sight, there is little evidence of any agricultural or other activity, it is the case that all land has some use to its proprietor and prior permission for access may have to be sought. At certain times of the year you may not be welcome for both agricultural and sporting reasons. It is useful to note the dates of the important seasons in the wild country areas of the United Kingdom:

**Lambing**—in the valleys around April and May.

**Grouse Shooting**—August 12th to December 10th.

**Deer Stalking**—July 1st to February 15th.

Additionally in deer stalking, long range, high velocity rifles are used which can be dangerous at very great distances.

In certain wild country areas there is a tradition of free access to the upland areas, and the problems of access are greater in the valleys and on the lower slopes. The valley floor and sides are enclosed by small fields which provide fodder and winter pasture. They are surrounded by the characteristic stone walls which should never be climbed. It is essential to use the 1:25000 *Pathfinder* or *Outdoor Leisure Maps* wherever possible, both for route planning and navigation, as the field boundaries are shown on maps of this scale. They also show the tracks and paths which give access to the more open terrain of the higher ground. Rights of way are clearly marked and paths are shown in greater detail which makes them easier to follow and so avoid damage or problems with the land owners.

Abroad, access to land, especially mountain and wilderness country, is usually much easier. Population densities are usually far less and there is not the same pressure on the land. On the other hand access to some localities, for example military areas, may be highly sensitive and reaction to intrusion may be dramatic and very direct. It is always wise to consult and be aware of local custom.

# Alternative Routes and Escape Routes

No matter how large a ship or aircraft is, navigation must always take the weather into consideration. You must plan with the weather in mind. Bad weather should be regarded as the norm in the mountains rather than the exception. The hill walker out for the day, when faced with foul weather may well decide to call it a draw and retire gracefully to the nearest hostelry. If it is essential that you reach your destination, in spite of the bad weather, then an alternative route may be the answer. A bad weather alternative route is a route which will enable you to reach your destination and yet avoid the worst of the weather. Usually this means keeping below the cloud base, or below the snow line, away from the full force of the elements on exposed ridges, or latching on to some line feature which will act as a handrail. Sometimes it may just involve following a clearly defined path, such as an old drove road, rather than making your way across country. Alternative routes usually add extra mileage to a journey as they involve going round rather than over.

## Escape Routes

An escape route, unlike a bad weather alternative route does not enable you to reach your destination; it only enables you to escape from the immediate predicament you are in. A North Westerly snow storm on the Cairngorm plateau may drive you to the sanctuary of the Shelter Stone on the lee side—but you still have problems!

Escape routes are usually safe ways of descending from the tops, paths which will enable you to get below the cloud base or away from the full force of the weather. You may well finish up on the wrong side of the hill or the wrong valley and be compelled to change your plans completely. If someone was expecting you at your destination you have a responsibility to get in touch with them as soon as possible.

## General Considerations

There are one or two other considerations worth taking into account before starting on the detail of the route:

## Duration

In our enthusiasm to see and do as much as possible, it is all too easy to be over-ambitious and plan too much into the time available. There should always be margins of time available to accommodate the unforeseen happening or the influence of the weather. This is particularly important where there is a dependence on public transport, or transport which is outside of your control. This may lead to forced marches or the taking of unjustifiable risks. Plan with the unexpected in mind and allow plenty of time for adjustment, or acclimatization, at your departure point and ample recovery time at your destination in case all does not go according to plan.

In expedition planning, having allowed sufficient time for the unexpected at the beginning and end of the journey, divide the journey evenly between the number of days available. This will prevent unreasonable demands being made on the body on a particular day, or days, which only results in over exhaustion or complaints such as blisters. This is particularly important in expeditions which only last a few days, and where expedition fitness is not acquired until near the end of the venture, if at all.

## Start Early in the Morning

If your journey is a lengthy one plan to start early in the morning as this will reduce your chances of being overtaken by darkness at the end of the day. This is particularly important during the winter months when the hours of daylight are limited, especially in higher latitudes.

## Make Major Ascents Early in the Day

If it is your intention to climb to the top of a peak, pass or even make a prolonged climb, plan to do it early in the day. You will be fresher physically. If the weather is hot then it will probably be cooler and less humid than later in the day. In settled weather during the summer, fair weather cumulus and even thunderstorms build up during the course of the day so that the conditions and the views may be better early on. Psychologically you will have the satisfaction of enjoying your lunch and the panorama in high places and the knowledge that

the rest of the journey will be downhill. Should the weather deteriorate at least you will be heading in the right direction with each hundred metres of descent helping to reduce the impact of the weather. Things have a tendency to go wrong towards the end of the day, so if you have done your climbing in the morning you will be able to sort yourself out more effectively in the lower terrain of the afternoon or evening.

## Estimating Journey Time

Central to all route planning is the need to estimate how much time the journey will take. The time that it takes to complete a journey depends on many factors, the more important of which are listed below. They are expressed in terms of the walker but they can apply to all who journey by their own physical effort, without motorized assistance, with a little adaptation. Cyclists, horse riders and the canoeist will find the majority of these factors influence their rate of progress.

■ Physical fitness, or the fitness of the least fit member of a group. If the journey or expedition is going to last longer than four or five days then fitness will be acquired during the first four or five days, after which the party will be expedition fit and have fewer problems. Blisters, fatigue and other physical problems tend to occur during the first few days of a journey.

■ The distance to be covered.

■ The height to be climbed.

■ The proportion of the journey that will take place on paths.

■ The type of terrain—cotton grass moor, peat hags, limestone turf, sand dunes, swamps, forest etc.

■ Conditions underfoot—sodden ground, snow or ice.

■ Weather conditions, strong winds, driving rain, sleet or snow.

■ Visibility.

With all these factors to be taken into account it may seem an impossible task to estimate journey time. Fortunately some of these factors cancel each other out, whilst others, such as the weather, are beyond our control. Expressed arithmetically, speed of travel seems to be reduced to the lowest common denominator. Past experience is your best guide to journey time in the future and that is why the emphasis throughout has been placed on noting journey times, especially if timing is related to terrain and conditions.

## Allowing for Height Climbed

It is always more difficult to estimate journey time in mountainous country and various formulae have been devised to assist in this process. The original rule was devised by Naismith, a Scottish mountaineer, in the last century and this will be as good a starting point as any other for your needs as it is uncomplicated and easy to use.

*" The type of terrain influences our speed of travel".*

154

For a fit hill walker:
**1.** Allow 1 hour for every 3 miles of horizontal distance to be covered.

**2.** Allow an additional 30 minutes for every 1000 feet of ascent.

Metricated and rounded off this becomes:
**1.** Allow 12 minutes per kilometre of horizontal distance.

**2.** Allow 10 minutes per 100 metres of ascent. (Or 1 minute per contour on fully metricated *Landranger* maps and fully metricated *Pathfinder*, and *Outdoor Leisure* maps in hilly and mountainous areas. In lowland areas the 1:25000 metricated maps have a 5 metre vertical interval).

For a fit hill walker, carrying a backpack with camping gear, the rule is:
**1.** Allow 1 hour for every $2\frac{1}{2}$ miles of horizontal distance.

**2.** Allow 1 hour for every 1500 feet to be climbed.

Metricated and rounded off this becomes:
**1.** Allow 15 minutes per kilometre of horizontal distance.

**2.** Allow 4 minutes for each 30 metres of ascent. (4 minutes for every 3 contours on the maps mentioned above).

This rule is no better, or worse, than any other rule for estimating journey time because only experience is a real guide to mastering this problem. Fig. 9.1. Use the rule as a basis for your calculations and then modify it in the light of your personal experience. Record your journey times and the modifications you make. There is no need to allow for descent. Walking gently down hill is pleasant but does not make a lot of difference to your travel time. Only when a descent becomes very steep, and you have to start picking your way, will it be necessary to make an additional time allowance.

If you find that you are always behind your estimated time then modify by adding another 5 minutes and allow 20 minutes for every

**FIG. 9.1** Allowing for height climbed

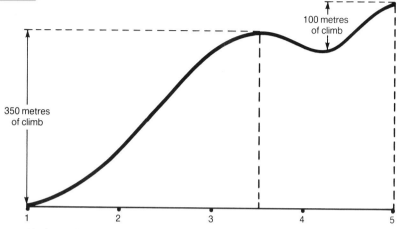

Horizontal distance 5 kms at 15 minutes per km = 75 mins
height climbed 350 m + 100 m = 450 m at 4 mins per 30
metres (15 × 4) = 60 mins.
Time to summit = 75 mins + 60 mins = 2 hrs 15 mins.

kilometre of horizontal distance with a pack on your back. If you think that it is walking uphill which puts you behind time, allow an extra minute or two for each 30 metres of height climbed. If you are always ahead of schedule clip a minute or two off until you get it right. If the figures are easy to remember and use, and the minutes related to the number of contours crossed, so much the better. It is a usual practice to add ten minutes per hour for a "breather" but you can use this time as "recovery time" until you get your estimations about right. Practice journeys are intended to sort these problems out.

## Planning the Route

If the journey is to last several days or longer, then your resting places for the nights will have an important role in the selection of your route. Accommodation is more easily found in the valleys and camp sites are usually located in the valley bottoms for shelter, supplies, easier access and communications. Alternatively, your purpose may be high level camping or the use of a mountain hut. These factors

alone may well determine your choice of route. If the ascent of a mountain, or a number of peaks, is your aim, after the selection of your departure and finishing points the route will be fairly well determined, but the height climbed must always be related to the horizontal distance travelled. It is helpful to take a piece of thin string and, using the linear scale on your map, cut off a length equal to the distance you wish to travel in a day. Lay this along your proposed route and then you can make any modifications you feel are necessary either to the distance or the amount of climbing. For fit young people covering a horizontal distance of 20 kilometres in a day, any route which involves more than 550 or 600 metres of ascent should be regarded with suspicion. During the winter months, especially with snow and ice, even these figures would be excessive.

Some mountain walkers have a good eye for selecting a natural line for a route on the map, partly instinctive and partly through experience, while others tend to choose unnatural and perverse routes. The good route will be well graded and conserve energy by avoiding unnecessary descents.

After you have planned your day's walk prepare a route card. Divide the day's journey into sections or legs. These legs should split the journey into natural divisions and, where possible, be marked by the principal checkpoints, or way marks, on the route. Sometimes the legs will be differentiated by a major change in direction, by ascent and descent or a change from one method of route finding to another, such as changing from following a path to climbing a gulley or using a compass to cross a featureless area of terrain. At other times the end of a leg may be marked by a meal break. Four to eight legs are usually a suitable number of divisions for a day's journey. Wherever your checkpoints are located, and whatever method you use for splitting your journey into legs, your checkpoints must be unmistakable. They must always be physical features on the ground which cannot be confused, for to navigate from a wrongly identified checkpoint is surely one of the most effective ways of losing yourself.

## The Route Card

The route card is an important document as it is a statement of your intentions. In preparing it you have had to sort out all your ideas and intentions and commit them to paper. If you have no clear idea of your intentions then you place yourself at a disadvantage from the start. Part of the Mountain Code is to tell someone where you are going so that in the event of an accident a mountain rescue team has some means of locating you. A copy of your route card will do this better than any other way. Another vital role of the route card is to act as a log of the journey. By making a note on the card of the times you reach the various checkpoints, and comparing them with the estimated times, you quickly acquire experience in how fast you travel over different kinds of country which can be used for future planning. You may even care to jot down the weather and conditions underfoot and you will then have an easily created log to be stored away for reference, which would do credit to a mariner.

Fig. 9.2 is a specimen route card. The first column presents no problem—the major checkpoints with their grid references. The second column headed "General Direction or Bearing" is more contentious. Many route cards head this column "Bearing". I believe that this is wrong! The intention of this column should be to indicate the general direction of travel which is best expressed by using the cardinal or inter-cardinal points. During a two year sojourn in Cumbria I had the opportunity to look at hundreds of route cards of young people engaged in mountain ventures in the Lake District. I was often appalled by what I saw, frequently finding bearings leading from the summit of Helvellyn to Patterdale. Any attempt to walk on such a bearing would be suicidal for it leads straight over the edge of the precipitous back wall of Red Tarn; it even goes through the tarn itself. Practically every venture, over the course of three or four days, would contain examples of similar, or greater, follies. The problem arises out of the habit of experienced hill walkers making a note of crucial bearings on their route, say from a summit to the ridge which they will use for their descent, to avoid having to do it with the wind

tearing the map out of their hands. These bearings usually extend only some hundreds of metres. The unknowing have turned a perfectly sound practice into a recipe for disaster—a literal example of Alexander Pope's warning that, "a little learning is a dang'rous thing;". If you are going to travel on a compass bearing across a plateau, open moorland or any other featureless terrain, by all means enter the bearing on your route card. If you wish to work out the bearing in the comfort of your home which will take you from the summit of Helvellyn to the start of Striding Edge in case you are enveloped in cloud, then do so by all means—it will certainly ensure that you are on the right path. You could even pencil in the number of paces required between the summit and the start of the ridge. But **never** write down a bearing for use in an emergency which cannot be followed.

All bearings entered on the route card must be magnetic bearings so that they can be used directly on the compass. Always adjust for magnetic variation immediately after you have taken the bearing from the map and then enter it on the card. So that you will form the habit of writing down the magnetic bearing, and to avoid confusion, write a capital "M" after the bearing.

The following columns are self-explanatory, providing the detail to work out the time taken to travel each leg. When the travelling time is added to the time of departure we have an Estimated Time of Arrival, or ETA, at our checkpoint; by adding the times for all the legs, and any breaks, we can work out an ETA at our final destination.

The column titled "Details of route" should indicate the method of route finding to be employed, e.g. Follow right of way, follow boundary wall or walk on bearing, to which local detail can be added.

Naismith's rule and its subsequent derivatives were devised to enable the hill walker to calculate the duration of a day's journey, and Naismith was the first to insist that it should not be used for calculating

159

# FIG. 9.2 Specimen Route Card and map

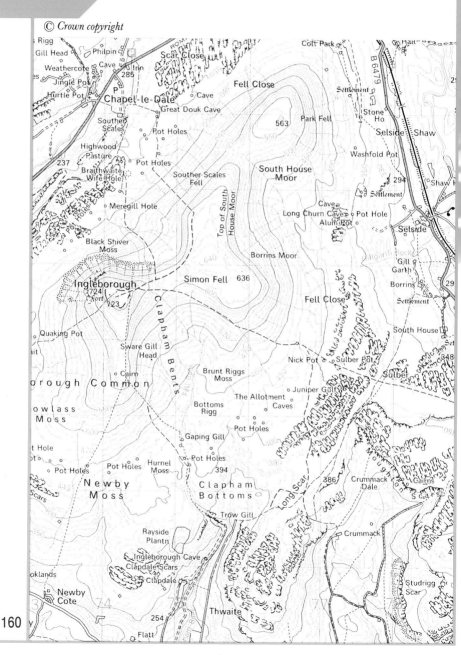

**ROUTE CARD** (Use one per day)

| Day of the week | Date | | NAMES OF GROUP MEMBERS | NAME OF GROUP OR UNIT |
|---|---|---|---|---|
| TUES | 7th JULY 1989 | | BARBARA MAIDMENT, MARTYN COX, PAUL RUSSELL, SUE SMITH, ELEANOR HANSON, MILFORD HINDMAN. | FOCUS YOUTH CLUB<br>ADDRESS RAILWAY APPROACH HAWORTH.<br>TEL. No. 019-315-205 |

Setting out time: 9.00 a.m.

| Leg | PLACE WITH GRID REF | Day of Venture 1st, 2nd etc | General Direction or bearing | Distance in km/miles | Height climbed in m/ft | Time allowed for leg | Time for stops or meals | Total time for leg | Estimated Time of Arrival E.T.A. | Details of route to be followed | Escape to: |
|---|---|---|---|---|---|---|---|---|---|---|---|
| START | SELSIDE 783755 | | | | | | | | | | |
| 1 | TO PATH Jct SULBER 777735 | | SW then S | 2.8 | 80 | 50 | 10 | 60 | 10.00 | Walled path towards Alum Pot then Gillgarth Beck, then path S to Sulber. | Return. |
| 2 | TO SHOOTING HUT 766739 | | W | 1.3 | 50 | 25 | 10 | 35 | 10.35 | Follow path by Sulber and Nick Pots, then by wall. | E to Horton. |
| 3 | TO INGLEBOROUGH 741745 | | W | 2.9 | 300 | 85 | 30 | 1.55 | 12.30 | Path to Allotment wall then across Simon Fell Breast to summit. | Return. |
| 4 | TO LITTLE INGLEBOROUGH 743735 | | E then S | 1.4 | — | 20 | 10 | 30 | 13.00 | Retrace path to Swine Tail then follow path towards Cairn. | Return by same route. |
| 5 | TO SWALLOW HOLE GREY WIFE SIKE 737723 | | between S and SW | 1.4 | — | 20 | 10 | 30 | 13.30 | Take SW fork at junction with Gaping Gill path. | South by same path. |
| 6 | TO NEWBY COTE 732705 | | between S and SW | 1.9 | — | 30 | 1 | 30 | 14.00 | Follow path or Sike bed. | South by same path. |
| 7 | TO | | | | | | | | | ALTERNATIVE ROUTE FOR BAD WEATHER. Follow proposed route to Sulber then path to Clapham and | |
| 8 | TO | | | | | | | | | Trow Gill, then Long Lane to then Old Road to Newby Cote. | |
| | Totals | | | 11.7 km | 430m | 3hr 50 | 1hr 10 | 5 hrs | 14.00 | | |

Supervisor's Name, Location, Tel No. 93-75205.
EVAN FERGESON, INGLETON YOUTH HOSTEL.
PETER PARFREY,

the time of journeys lasting only a part of a day. They are no use for preparing time-tables of movements through the mountains. Though the timings appear to have the precision of a railway time-table it is an illusion; there are far too many unknowns in mountain walking. They are a statement of intent and, though the course of the journey may be followed diligently, anyone who hopes to make contact with a group at a certain time, must always wait in hope rather than expectation.

## SUMMARY

The most important consideration in all route planning is to plan a route which will fulfil the aims and objectives of the journey. The route must be within the capability of the participants and routes must take weather conditions into consideration.

Alternative routes which will enable the destination to be reached in bad weather by going "through" or "round", or which may be more clearly defined and easier to follow, should always be considered. Escape routes may enable you to avoid a particular hazard but prevent you from reaching your destination, which may give cause for concern. Plan for the unexpected and allow ample margins of time at the beginning and end of journeys.

Groups of young people engaged in mini-expeditions tend to process across the country at about 2.5 kilometres per hour ($1\frac{1}{2}$ mph); a journey of 20 kilometres (12 miles) takes around 8 hours.

To be able to provide realistic Estimated Time of Arrival (ETA) journey times should always be recorded. In mountainous terrain particular attention should be paid to the extra time needed to make ascents and to devise a formula which will suit your needs. Do not include any bearing on a route card which cannot be followed in its entirety.

# CHAPTER 10

# NAVIGATION IN
# RESTRICTED VISIBILITY

The two major factors which limit visibility are atmospheric conditions and darkness. Vegetation, particularly woodland and forest, can also present navigational problems but, since vegetation is associated with the type of terrain, it is probably more appropriate to consider it separately later on.

The navigational problems created by atmospheric conditions and darkness arise because they isolate navigators from their reference points, the landmarks and features on which they depend to establish their position. Deprived of external reference features for direction and position they have to rely on a self-centred system, the compass, for direction which is not as accurate, is more complex and time consuming in use, and makes it more difficult to establish position with any degree of accuracy. This increases the probability of the navigator moving, or straying, into a dangerous area. The results can be the same on land, sea or in the air; the weekend sailor finishing up on a half-tide rock, the light aircraft crashing into high ground or the hill walker going over the edge of a cliff or straying into an avalanche area. Amongst novices and the less experienced, the sense of mental isolation may create stress and anxiety which is more inhibiting than the actual geographical isolation. Finding your way in restricted visibility is as much about confidence as technique, but the confidence can only come through well-practised techniques. Darkness and atmospheric conditions, though they both restrict our ability to see, are obviously different in nature and each presents different problems.

## Atmospheric Conditions

The most frequent condition, especially for the mountain walker, which restricts visibility is cloud or hill-fog, but snow can be just as restrictive. Rain, unless it is of the torrential kind usually associated with a thunderstorm, does not normally present a problem. In some parts of the world wind-driven dust and sand make navigation difficult. Blizzard conditions, heavy snow driven by gale force winds, probably present the most severe problems especially when the wind is whipping up the surface snow to give the almost impossible

conditions of a "white-out"; although white-outs can occur under different weather conditions.

Cloud, fog and hill-fog are all the same, tiny drops of water, about a micron (0.001 mm) in diameter, which sink imperceptibly, or remain suspended in the air. The droplets may be larger but at around 100 microns (0.1 mm) in diameter they may fall as drizzle, and as rain when the diameter is about a millimetre. The size of the droplets and their concentration, which may reach many hundreds, or even thousands, per cubic centimetre, determine how thick the fog or cloud is and the extent to which visibility is reduced. When these conditions occur in contact with the ground we use the word fog for lower ground, cloud or hill-fog for higher ground, but it is largely a matter of semantics. Mist is thin fog while the term haze is used for the obscuration associated with dust, smoke and the effects of heat. The meteorologist's definition of fog is when atmospheric conditions reduce surface visibility to less than one kilometre; while this may have a profound influence on the navigation of a ship or plane it is not likely to inconvenience the walker; only when visibility drops below 200 metres does route finding become more difficult unless the terrain is particularly featureless. Mountains make their own weather and clouds and mountains go together. It is the cooling of the air as it is forced to rise over hills and mountains which condenses the water vapour into the droplets which form much of the cloud in these areas; though of course, clouds are frequently formed in other ways in mountainous areas. If you go into the mountains frequently then you will encounter clouds for they are part of the mountain scene.

## Navigation in Cloud or Fog

There are a number of simple precautions which we can take to make route finding in fog a manageable activity. The most important point to make is that we should never be taken unawares. We can see the cloud moving towards us, or fog rolling over the ground in our direction. We know when we are going to move into cloud, usually by ascending above the cloud base. Clouds in general, and stratus clouds in particular, tend to keep to a fairly constant height with a cloud base which is usually fairly easy to discern. Over a period of time the cloud

base may tend to lift which may indicate an improvement in both the weather and visibility, while a lowering cloud base usually indicates that the weather is closing in and conditions are worsening. If there is a cloud base it is important to keep an eye on what it is doing even though it may remain at the same height all day. Clouds often have a discernible pattern. They frequently sit on the tops of hills or mountains while occasionally we see a banner cloud streaming from the lee side of a mountain. It is easy to determine the height of the cloud base if we can find a feature on or just below the cloud base which is marked on the map—we just read off the height from the contours. Sometimes the cloud base will conveniently rest on the top of one of the lower hills with a Spot Height.

The first thing to do before the hill fog reaches you, or you reach the hill fog, is to stop. If your objective is within sight and a compass course would provide a safe and reasonable method of reaching it, get out your compass and take a bearing on the objective in the same way as you would check the direction of a path. Do this before it is swallowed up in the cloud. You can then walk on the bearing to your objective. Whether you are able to do this or not, get out the map and make sure that you are certain of your position. Then have a very careful look around the landscape—it may be the last you will see of it for quite a while. In conjunction with the map make a mental note of any hazards in your vicinity. Then see if you can tighten up your route finding and lift your general level of awareness. If you are just finding your own route across open country you may be able to find a footpath which will take you to where you want to go. If you are already on a footpath which is not very well defined you could possibly locate one of the well worn tracks. If there are no paths consider if any line features, such as a stream or a boundary wall, will act as a handrail and take you towards your objective or possibly below the cloud level if that is your desire. If these options are not available then get out the compass straight away, don't wait until you are lost, and work out the bearing to your objective while you still know your position. Pay particular attention to distance. If you have practised the compass techniques of Chapter 8 in the conditions suggested, you will find little

*"Clouds and mountains go together".*

difficulty in holding your course, but distance is difficult to estimate in limited visibility. In daylight, visibility in fog will rarely, if ever, drop below 50 metres and is more likely to remain around 100 metres or more. This will enable you to fix your eyes on a spot on the ground and maintain a sufficiently accurate course. If you are on a path it is worth while checking its direction occasionally with your compass and pay particular attention at path intersections.

If the clouds should part and your objective is revealed, make the most of the opportunity for it may not last for more than a brief moment and seconds may be precious. If it is possible to follow a compass bearing, take a bearing straight away or check your existing one. Take careful note of the surrounding terrain and make a note of any potential hazards and any features which may assist you in locating your objective if the cloud should return.

If you are travelling uphill to the top of a peak remember that your problems may occur later when you try to find your way down. As you will recall from Chapter 6 "up" is one of the easiest directions to

follow, while coming down can present all kinds of difficulties, not only in our navigation, but because our movements tend to be less secure when travelling downwards.

If cloud is sitting on the top of the mountains or the weather particularly bad, you may well decide on an alternative route if you do not feel that your navigation is up to the task; go through, or go round rather than over. Travelling while enveloped in cloud is a taste which not everyone acquires.

Fog forms in the valleys and on low ground under stable weather conditions frequently in the evenings and early mornings during anticyclonic conditions, and especially during the spring and autumn. This radiation and advection fog, rarely poses route-finding problems in the British Isles. It may be a wise precaution to have a compass in fenland areas, but abroad, large areas of marsh or swampland can provide a severe test of your ability to use the compass.

During daylight hours fog has one advantage; you can at least see where you are putting your feet.

## Navigation in the Dark

The vast majority of the population in the British Isles is deprived of darkness. There are lights everywhere and the lights of our towns and cities switch themselves on at the onset of twilight or the least reduction in daylight and burn all night. One of the most marked changes a night traveller on the continent notices is the vast difference in the level of artificial illumination at night between most of Britain and the lower levels of the continent. This continually high level of illumination inevitably leads many people to regard darkness as an alien environment, which is at the best strange and at the worst frightening, instead of a perfectly natural phenomenon. This places many at a disadvantage from the outset when it comes to finding their way in the dark.

Though the navigational problems and solutions associated with darkness are the same as with fog, the characteristics are different.

*"Sometimes the cloud base will rest on the top of one of the lower hills".*

The onset of darkness is predictable, give or take a little. Its duration varies with latitude and with the season of the year. Both its onset and duration can be found for any latitude and longitude years in advance so there is little excuse for anyone being taken by surprise. In the latitudes of the British Isles there is a very marked difference in the hours of darkness between summer and winter and between the South Coast and the far North of Scotland. The hours of darkness in winter may place a severe restriction on the time available for ventures, especially in northern Scotland, and increase the probability of benightment. A good diary and a table of "lighting up times" are adequate for most planning purposes, or you may consult a copy of *The Nautical Almanac* (HMSO) or the compact *Reeds Nautical Almanac* in your local library.

Darkness is not total or absolute; total darkness in the natural world is usually reserved for cavers and potholers without lights. Even after the sun has set it continues to provide illumination by reflection from the upper layers of the earth's atmosphere—twilight. There are three twilights, civil, nautical and astronomical. Civil twilight lasts from sunset until the sun is 6 degrees below the horizon and there is officially deemed to be sufficient light to work out of doors. Nautical twilight continues until the sun is 12 degrees below the horizon and marks the

169

end of the time when sailors can make their sextant observations on the stars and the four "navigational planets". Astronomical twilight extends until the sun is 18 degrees below the horizon and there is a period in summer when the sun is never more than 18 degrees below the horizon from any place in the British Isles—"twilight all night". Even at midnight the northern sky is illuminated by the scattered light from the sun. This period increases with latitude and is most obvious in the North of Scotland. Darkness will not reach a maximum until after the end of astronomical twilight. The moon, even a new or old moon, provides a significant amount of light, and again the information is readily available in a diary. There is far more light available than many city dwellers imagine and nearly always enough to find one's way.

There is a problem which occurs from time to time; while it is frequently easy to see the outline, or even detail of the land, several kilometres away, it is sometimes difficult to see where you are placing your feet. Our eyes automatically adjust to the low levels of light available at night, but it takes a considerable time for this adjustment to take place. At the end of fifteen minutes the eyes will have made a considerable adjustment but the improvement in night vision will continue for the better part of an hour. This night sight can be destroyed immediately by the flash of a torch in our eyes and it will take a long time before it is regained! It is essential to keep any light used for map reading, or using the compass, to the absolute minimum and always directed away from the eyes. Some close one eye.

On the darkest of nights it may be necessary to use light to see where we are placing our feet, especially on steep or rocky terrain, bog, swamp or snow and ice. The light should always be pointed down and kept to the minimum. There is another school of thought—flooding the whole area with the light from miners' or cavers' headlamps or carrying mini searchlights. You need to go out at night and find out for yourself. See how long your eyes take to adjust to the dark. Find out if you need a torch to place your feet and appreciate what effect the torch has on your eyes. Learn to control the use of light for map

reading, compass work and movement over the ground. My personal preference has always been to try and manage without a light whenever possible and always use the minimum amount of light when this is impossible. If you use excessive light you will inevitably surround yourself with a wall of darkness at the end of your torch beam.

If you are overtaken by darkness adopt the same solutions as you would for cloud or fog. Though nightfall is inevitable it can still catch you unawares, especially in winter and when the weather is bad or there is a thick blanket of cloud. Take action while there is still some light left; by getting a move on it may be possible to negotiate a particularly difficult or steep area of terrain while there is still daylight available. Many parties of novices dawdle along during the late afternoon and show no urgency until it is too late. Do not be panicked by the onset of darkness and throw caution to the winds; most falls occur during descents—just keep on moving steadily along. Locate your position carefully and look around. If you are in the mountains then, in all probability, you will be descending so choose a route, if possible, which will take you clear of difficult terrain. See if there is a well-used path or track within reach which will not only solve your route finding problems but make your footwork so much easier and certain. If there is no path to follow, consider if there is a natural feature leading in your direction which you can utilize. Work out any bearing which you may need while there is still daylight left and you can still locate your position. The compass techniques you practised in the dark will be adequate for your needs. As the darkness increases in many areas of England, Wales, Northern Ireland, and the southern half of Scotland you may have the glow of lights from distant towns and cities to act as navigation beacons, often visible over twenty, thirty or more miles away. Check their direction with your compass and use them to orient yourself—you do not even have to be able to identify them. Television and radio masts often carry very bright warning lights for aircraft which are visible over long distances. As in fog, pay close attention to distance and the direction of paths. Maintain a high level of concentration, for features can be overlooked in the dark and

it is all too easy to relax concentration at the end of a tiring day when you think that the worst of the journey is over; often with disastrous consequences.

Your skills should be sufficient to enable you to cope with cloud/fog and darkness. By themselves neither of these natural phenomena should present any real difficulty for this is why you bought a compass and learnt how to use it by practising in woods and in the dark. You may not deliberately seek these conditions in the mountains or wilderness country but, if they are forced upon you, you should be able to get by.

Unfortunately these conditions can be cumulative; it may be dark with thick fog; it may be dark with thick fog and storm force winds driving heavy snow and it may be impossible even to see your feet. Under these conditions in the mountains movement may become virtually impossible and it is necessary to sit it out until conditions improve and trust that your emergency equipment is up to its task. The wise mountain walker is the one who, while extending his experience, can balance it against the conditions likely to be encountered. If you wish to set yourself a target of competence for navigation in restricted visibility, practise until you can cope with darkness and fog together.

## Forests

Forests and tall vegetation, not only restrict visibility, but they obviously physically impede movement. Progress may be slowed, not only by the need to use the compass but by overcoming the obstructions and making detours. Deciduous woodland and natural coniferous forest is usually too difficult and progress can be made. Densely planted forest can be very difficult and the best advice to those intending to navigate in them is, don't—use the breaks or rides. Woodland provides an excellent initial training ground for using the compass and should present few problems. Sight on some mark in the usual way and then move towards it, avoiding the obstacles in your path. You will soon develop the ability to keep one eye on your target and the other on the obstruction in your path. At night it may be necessary to use a technique from Chapter 13.

*"The onset of darkness is predictable".*

## SUMMARY

Cloud or fog, along with darkness, are the two major factors in restricting visibility, though blizzards and vegetation can also cause problems.

Cloud or hill fog rarely reduces visibility to less than some 50 or 100 metres in daylight and then it is possible to use the compass effectively by sighting on some spot on the ground. Try to avoid being taken by surprise and, where possible, follow a clearly defined path or line feature and pay careful attention to distance travelled.

The onset of darkness is predictable and should not catch anyone unawares. There is usually sufficient light to navigate by, but a torch is necessary to read the map and may be necessary to see where to place one's feet. Great care is necessary when using lights to avoid destroying night-vision.

Losing yourself and finding yourself again is all part of the process of learning to navigate. The learning comes from locating your position after you have gone astray. Knowing where you are is a relative state. One place on a featureless moor is very like another and may be of no more importance; the only thing of importance is that having crossed that featureless moor you are on course and heading for your objective. From listening to the accounts of the journeys of some young people, many succeed in reaching their destination without ever realising that they were lost for part of the day—lost in the sense that they were not where they thought they were. For many, being lost, remote from human habitation, with nightfall imminent can be a traumatic experience. Cloud or hill-fog enhances the isolation and the presence of precipitous slopes in the vicinity, real or imagined, can, in some cases, create such a state of anxiety that further movement becomes impossible. There comes a time when weather conditions are so difficult, that common sense demands it is wiser to go to ground and wait for an improvement rather than carry on. Unfortunately, some parties throw in the towel and sit around, tired and demoralized, waiting to be rescued in broad daylight when it is possible to see for miles. They are lost, their map reading skills are inadequate to locate themselves, they have not the confidence and resolution to use the compass, and frequently seem to lack the mental ability to sort out their navigational problems. Any group which gets itself into such a situation has a responsibility to get itself out again. Sorting yourself out when you are lost is rather like detective work—a mixture of careful observation and applied intelligence.

It is possible to devise a procedure which you can use if, or when, you get lost. The procedure must suit you and your way of thinking; the method is not important but it is necessary that you give thought to the problem before it occurs. It must be a method for the mountains or wilderness country; we are not talking about getting lost in greenfield country, the local wood, heath, forest or chase.

When lost, the first and most important step is to try and find out where you are and the second is to plan a route which will take you to your original destination. Finding out where you are is the hard part.

It is easy to travel considerable distances in wild country before realizing that you are lost. Some never realize that they are lost until they arrive at the wrong place; they see the name of the village beside the road in the wrong valley. At least their problems of relocation have been solved. You may reach your presumed destination expecting to find a bothy only to encounter a reservoir; your route finding is all right but your map is out of date. In unfamiliar country it is very easy to arrive at the correct location and yet fail to identify it. Instances of this kind are the exception; usually the realization that something is amiss dawns much more slowly, a vague uneasiness, expected landmarks do not turn up, the spur seems to be leading in the wrong direction. How soon you realize you are off course will depend on your observation and alertness, but the sooner you are aware the easier the situation can be corrected. You may well save yourself a lot of

*"One place on a featureless moor is very much like another".*

physical effort and wasted time which may become very important at the end of the day.

The procedure I have always taught is based on asking yourself a series of questions—they may not always enable you to find out where you are, but they should enable you to take the most appropriate course of action in your predicament. The procedure was devised to enable teachers and youth leaders to provide the young people in their care with a more systematic way of coping with being lost, rather than just wandering around hopefully. It was intended for novices but you may find it helpful to use this procedure until experience provides you with your own way of dealing with the situation.

Before considering the procedure in detail let us look at the logic behind it.

If, on leaving your departure point A, you fail to reach your objective B it can only be due to one of two navigational reasons:

either
■ You have travelled in the wrong direction.

or
■ You have not travelled the correct distance—you have not travelled far enough, or you have passed your objective without realizing it.

This is based on the assumption that your departure point has been correctly identified. In wild country this can be a problem, one spur or one re-entrant can look very much like another. If your departure point was incorrect then you can only reach your objective by accident—by travelling in the wrong direction.

It is also reasonable to assume that the failure to reach your destination is to be found in the method of route finding you were using at the time; your method of route finding was not appropriate for the terrain or the prevailing weather conditions. If you were following a path, you followed the wrong path; if you were walking on a bearing you

strayed off course, or more probably you did not travel far enough—it is very easy to over-estimate the distance travelled when using a compass in bad visibility. The path may have been obscured by snow and you should have used the compass rather than hoping to find it further on.

The following six or seven questions are designed to take these factors into account. Use this procedure until you can devise one of your own which is more suited to your needs and experience.

At the first indication of being lost or the first feelings of uneasiness:

**Stop and Make a Note of the Time.**

**Set your Map** using the compass if necessary.

**While Comparing Map and Country** ask yourself the following questions. The order in which you ask the questions is not vital after the first two. Their purpose is to try and provide that vital clue to your location or, failing that, direct your attention to the area into which you have most probably strayed; "the area of probability."

### ■ Why do I think I am lost?

Usual answers are: The path/valley/spur is leading me in the wrong direction. I should have passed the Shooting Box ages ago. This question must come first because you, for a host of different reasons, may be in the right place but fail to recognize it. The shooting box was burnt down in 1902, the expected stream or moorland tarn has dried up in the hot weather. Try and eliminate this possibility first. Remember maps are out-of-date from the moment they are made. If you feel that the path, valley or spur is leading you in the wrong direction check the direction with the compass. Sometimes if it is possible to improve your view of the landscape by moving 100 metres or so it may be worth while, but further travel will almost certainly make the situation more confusing and harder to resolve. Often the problem is far simpler—you have encountered a landmark or feature which you did not anticipate. Then ask yourself:

## ■ Where am I?

Compare your surroundings with the area of the map where you think you should be. If you have encountered an unexpected landmark or feature and it can be identified on the map your problems are solved. If not, see if there is a footpath, valley or spur marked on the map in the vicinity which has the direction indicated by your compass. By comparing the contours carefully with the terrain you may be able to relocate yourself. If you are successful you are no longer lost! All that remains to be done is work out a fresh route to your original objective. If you are unable to relocate yourself ask the next question.

**FIG. 11.1** Why do I think I am lost?

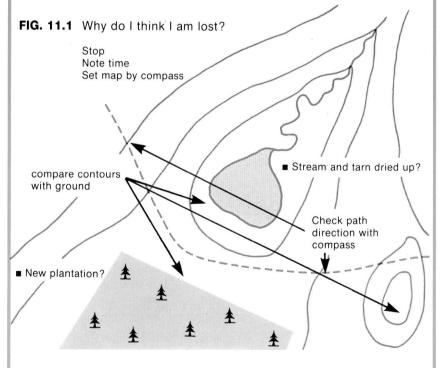

Stop
Note time
Set map by compass

compare contours
with ground

■ Stream and tarn dried up?

Check path
direction with
compass

■ New plantation?

You may be in the correct place but fail to recognize it?
Map out of date? Building, forestry or agricultural development?
Alterations due to prevailing weather conditions?
Look at landform and shape.

## ■ How far have I travelled?

The answer to this question can only be worked out from the time which has elapsed since you left your last checkpoint or were able to pinpoint your position with certainty; unless you were pacing. Having noted the time when you thought you were lost, subtract the time at your last checkpoint. Calculate the maximum distance you could have travelled in the time. A circle with a radius of the maximum distance drawn on the map around your last positive position will contain your position. You do not have to actually draw a circle on the map, use your measure or compass base to mark off the distance in all the probable or possible directions. Concentrate your attention within this area and have another try at locating your position. Fig. 11.2.

**FIG. 11.2** How far have I travelled?

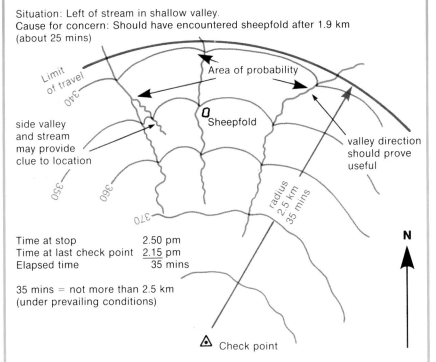

Situation: Left of stream in shallow valley.
Cause for concern: Should have encountered sheepfold after 1.9 km (about 25 mins)

Limit of travel

Area of probability

Sheepfold

side valley and stream may provide clue to location

valley direction should prove useful

radius 2.5 km 35 mins

| | |
|---|---|
| Time at stop | 2.50 pm |
| Time at last check point | 2.15 pm |
| Elapsed time | 35 mins |

35 mins = not more than 2.5 km
(under prevailing conditions)

N

Check point

181

*"The number of paths on the map may not correspond to the number on the ground"*.

## ■ How did I get lost?

The purpose of this question is to direct attention to the method of route finding, out of which your problem must have arisen. If your intention was to follow a spur down from the summit and the ridge you are following is now leading in a different direction to your objective then you must have followed the wrong spur. Many upland areas consist of dissected plateaux where it is very easy, when on the tops, especially in bad visibility, to confuse one valley or spur leading to lower ground with another. See fig. 11.3. It is all too easy to veer to the wrong side of a spur. Strong winds, especially if accompanied by driving rain or snow, can drive the most determined navigator off course for the desire to turn away from the weather can be almost irresistible, either to get it on your back or unconsciously seek the shelter of the lee slope. If you were walking on a bearing the problem may lie either in a failure to hold your course or in the distance travelled. Fig. 11.4. This question immediately leads on to the next.

182

**FIG. 11.3** How did I get lost?

Must be in method of route-finding! Followed wrong spur, valley, path, wrong bearing, incorrect distance?

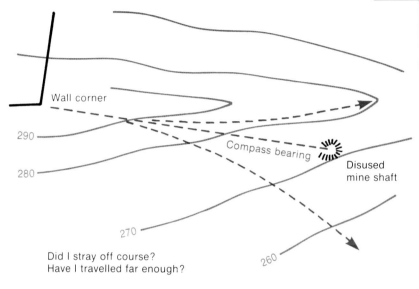

Did I stray off course?
Have I travelled far enough?

**FIG. 11.4** How did I get lost?

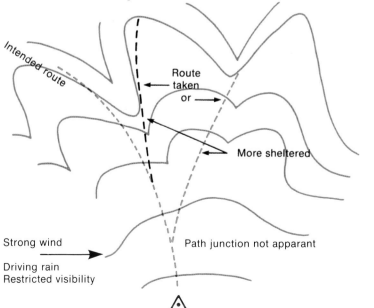

183

### ■ Where did I get lost?

Having decided how you got lost, it is frequently possible to find out where you went wrong. If you were following a path the chances are that you either set out on the wrong path or you mistook a path at an intersection. It is often difficult to relate the paths on the ground to those on the map, sometimes there are far too many on the ground especially in popular areas, while at other times the paths may be hardly discernible. Remember that man is not the only creature to make paths, animals have realized their advantages for as long as we have. Soil creep and grazing sheep together give rise to the terracettes which are a feature of the steeper slopes of many of our upland areas.

**FIG. 11.5** Where did I get lost?

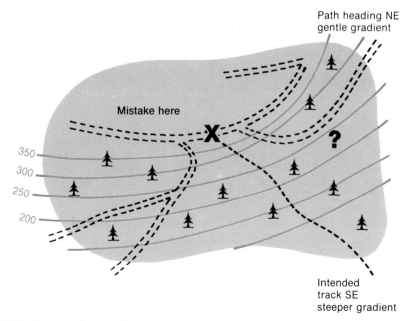

Path heading NE
gentle gradient

Mistake here

350
300
250
200

?

Intended
track SE
steeper gradient

Thick pine forest, steep slope.
Worth retracing steps to correct
mistake.

If you were following a natural linear feature such as a ridge, spur or valley then the mistake probably occurred in the approach to the feature. If you are able to identify the location of your mistake then, providing it is not too far away, it may be worth while retracing your steps and returning to your original route. Remember the emphasis placed in the earlier chapters on the level of alertness and observation required to perform this task. If the mistake occurred a considerable distance away, or to return would involve a prolonged climb, then it may be necessary to seek an alternative solution. If you have a good idea of where you went wrong, and of the path or feature you followed in mistake, it should lead to finding the area in which you are located and prove of considerable assistance. Fig. 11.5.

These five questions should have enabled you to relocate yourself or they should, at least, have narrowed down the area in which you are lost. There is a sixth question you can consider before asking the last and most important question.

*"Terracettes—a combination of soil creep, grazing sheep with human assistance".*

### ■ Did I start from the right place?

If you have to ask this question you have problems! Previous chapters have stressed the need to have checkpoints which are as near to being unmistakable as humanly possible. If you suspect that your departure point was wrong and you have only been travelling for a short while, then it may be wise to retrace your route and relocate your departure point and then plan a fresh route from there. If not, then the area in which you are lost may be increased severalfold.

### ■ What action should I take?

There are five possible solutions to your situation:

**1.** If you have been able to relocate yourself, all that is required is to plot a new route to your objective.

**2.** Retrace your route to your last checkpoint or where you went wrong and continue on your original route.

**3.** Carry on the way you are going.

**4.** Follow a natural feature such as a stream, river or valley which will usually, sooner or later, lead to habitation.

**5.** Use your compass to travel on a bearing from the area in which you are most probably lost, to a collecting feature such as a metalled track or road which forms the boundary to the area of mountain or wild country you are in.

The first solution does not require further comment. Retracing your route to the last checkpoint, or where you went wrong, is worth serious consideration, especially if the terrain is not too difficult, steep, or you have not too far to travel. Observant persons should not have much difficulty in retracing their steps along the paths or line features which are so often used, and there will be the advantage of returning to the original and preferred route. Only you can decide in the light of your situation.

The third solution, carry on the way you are going, may be forced upon you because you may be on a ridge or in a steep ravine which

186

may prevent any travel other than backwards or forwards. You must decide which is the better alternative. If you decide to go on then you will have to wait until you reach a suitable location before taking action to find out where you are or the "area of probability".

The fourth way, following a natural feature such as spur, valley or stream, may have to be considered. Streams are powerful indicators of direction, they lead inevitably to lower ground. If you are on high ground they can be most effective in leading you below the cloud base and into less extreme conditions. Following streams in steep terrain can be a dangerous practice especially for the inexperienced; for we all know of places where they disappear over a cliff (see Part 4). Following a stream or a valley in lower ground may be a solution to your problem, but you may have to travel a considerable distance before you are able to find habitation and the feature may be leading you further and further away from your original destination. If you

*"Streams lead to lower ground but walkers should keep clear of the gullies".*

use this solution do not follow the feature blindly, keep map and compass to hand so that you will be able to establish your position at the earliest opportunity. You can of course use a natural feature to lead to lower ground and better visibility where you may be able to locate your position without any difficulty.

The fifth method is frequently a solution to the situation. In Chapter 7 we considered the need to establish a reference frame around the area of your activity; unmistakable physical boundaries which cannot be crossed by accident such as roads, metalled tracks or rivers. These can now be used as back-stops, collecting features which you can aim for. If you do not know where you are it is impossible to work out a bearing which will take you to a precise destination, but you can obtain a bearing from an area of probability which will enable you to hit a road several miles long.

There are two parts to the solution:

(a) Finding the most probable area in which you are lost.
Using the answers to the questions above:
How far have I travelled?
How did I get lost?
Where did I get lost?
Did I start from the right place?

*"Unmistakable boundaries which cannot be crossed by accident such as roads".*

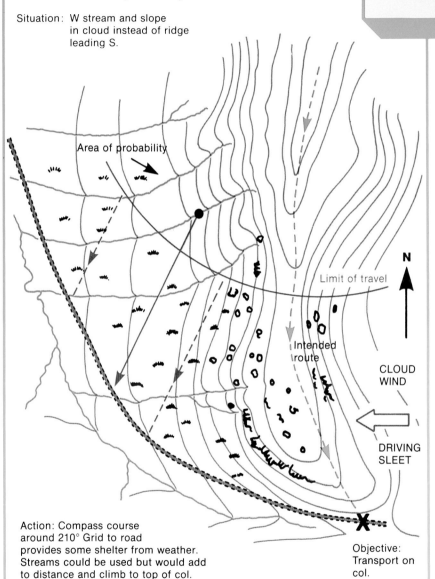

**FIG. 11.6** Area of probability.

Situation: W stream and slope
in cloud instead of ridge
leading S.

Area of probability

Limit of travel

N

Intended
route

CLOUD
WIND

DRIVING
SLEET

Action: Compass course
around 210° Grid to road
provides some shelter from weather.
Streams could be used but would add
to distance and climb to top of col.

Objective:
Transport on
col.

If you fail to locate your position:
Decide on the area in which you are most probably located
by suggested procedure.
Travel on compass bearing taken from centre of presumed
area to boundary or collecting feature.

Use Fig. 11.6 as an example to work out the area of probability and mark it on your map. Select your most probable location within that area and mark it, or alternatively mark the centre of the area.

(**b**) Select the most suitable part of the boundary to aim for. In England and Wales it is very difficult to be more than eight kilometres, or five miles, from a metalled road if this is any consolation, but this is not so in Scotland and other parts of the world. The nearest road may not always be the most suitable target. Weather, major obstacles and the difficulty of the terrain are usually deciding factors. You may not wish to climb over a pass or col or upwards into the cloud. Select a possible target area and then, using your map, examine the terrain for major obstacles between your area of probability and the target. If it looks very difficult move your target area to a different, and more suitable, place on the road or collecting feature, or try another direction altogether.

Having decided on your target area, work out the compass bearing from the place you marked within the area of probability. Then travel on that bearing and trust your compass. Do not change your mind again unless, while following the bearing, you are able to pinpoint your position beyond all reasonable doubt. It may then be possible to plan a more suitable route.

If you do get lost in bad conditions, in a remote place, try and keep your cool! Do not go rushing off in all directions and if, as is most likely, you are in a party, stay together. If it is panic stations—have your panic, then have a drink from your flask or brew up before settling down and fettling yourselves. This will be considerably easier if you have given the possibility of being lost some thought beforehand and devised a procedure for resolving the problem. Part 4 may also assist with techniques which could be of use in this situation.

**FIG. 11.7** On being Lost. Question and action chart

Stop – note time
Set map using compass – compare map and country

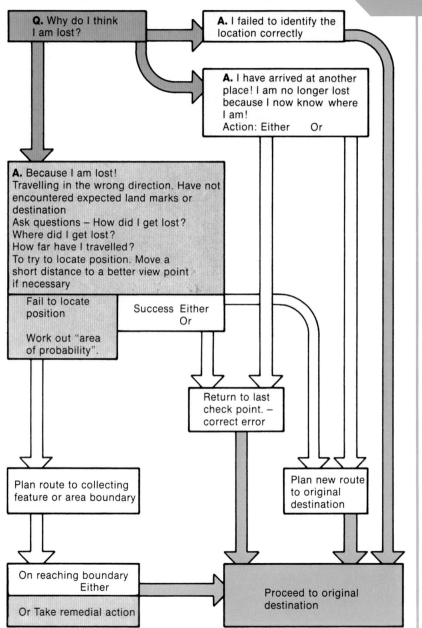

191

SUMMARY

Being lost is a learning situation. The time to think about being lost is before you are lost! It is possible to devise a procedure which will help in such a situation.

The routine suggested is based on asking yourself a series of questions which should either enable you to establish your location or, at least, narrow down the area where you are lost to "an area of probability" which will provide the opportunity to aim for a boundary, or collecting feature, by using the compass.

# PART 4

EXTENDING
YOUR SKILLS

# CHAPTER 12

## MORE WAYS
## WITH THE MAP

## Making Things Easy

The shortest distance between two places is not always the quickest, and it is rarely the most suitable, route. You do not have to travel to tropical rain forest to prove this point, there are many areas of millstone grit moor in Derbyshire or Yorkshire with their peat hags, cloughs and "bobbies' helmets"—the local name in the Dales for the hummocks or tufts of vegetation which cover miles of moorland and make walking exceedingly difficult. It is often better to travel further to make the walking less physically demanding; experience is the only guide to how much further it is worth travelling to obtain these benefits. When an opportunity arises to travel directly across country to your objective or take a more roundabout route with the use of a path or track, go one way and come back the other way, comparing the travelling times and the physical effort involved. A path or track makes for easier and less tiring walking, enabling the legs to be swung and a more even pace to be maintained. Less attention is needed as to where you place your feet and travelling time is more easily predicted. In restricted visibility these advantages become even more pronounced.

## Contouring

Contouring is a common method of conserving energy employed by those who travel in hilly country, and many of our footpaths employ this method of reducing physical effort to a greater or lesser extent. The extra distance of going round at a constant height is traded against the physical effort of having to go up and down, or down and up. Again, personal experience is the only guide to which is the better choice of route. Locate a suitable spur and a re-entrant and find out for yourself, noting the time and the physical effort involved.
Fig. 12.1

Other factors may influence your decision apart from the actual height which has to be climbed; the steepness of the terrain, whether you are backpacking or the difficulty of navigation. If it means going round the head of a valley or ravine then it is usually possible to establish a point to aim for on the other side and route finding presents no problems. If, on the other hand, you are travelling round a spur it

**FIG. 12.1**  Contouring

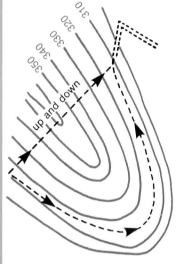

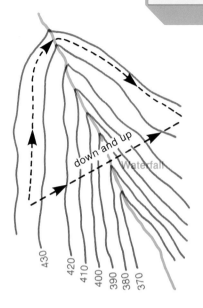

Going round to avoid climbing or
difficult terrain

may be difficult to establish your position on the other side without the
aid of an altimeter.

## Reaching Your Objective

Following footpaths and line features not only makes travel less
physically demanding, it forms the basis of much of our route finding.
We string a number of them together to form a route to our destination.
Even though it is not always possible to find paths or line features to
lead us to our destination it is nearly always possible to simplify the
route finding.

## Point to Point

In open country it is often possible to find a series of landmarks or
features which are easily visible from each other which will take us to
our destination; "point to point" navigation. This method of route
finding is particularly useful when crossing from one valley to another
because it is possible to head for a point on the skyline and from there
actually to be able to see our objective.

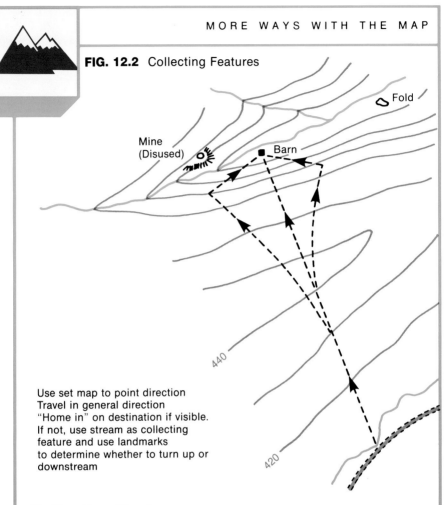

**FIG. 12.2** Collecting Features

Use set map to point direction
Travel in general direction
"Home in" on destination if visible.
If not, use stream as collecting
feature and use landmarks
to determine whether to turn up or
downstream

## Collecting Features

Your shelter for the night is a barn on the other side of a featureless
moor Fig. 12.2. Rather than resorting to walking on a bearing in good
visibility, it is easier to travel in the general direction of the valley,
which will act as a collecting feature. If you have held your course the
barn may be in sight as you descend to the valley and all you need to
do is make a "visual approach". If the barn is not visible on reaching
the valley, use your map to locate your position in the valley and then
move up or down stream to sight the barn. This is one of the oldest
techniques in navigation and has been used by sailors ever since man
has sailed out of sight of land. On making a landfall the sailor locates
his position by local knowledge or from the charts, which are designed
to meet this need, and then turns to left or right to reach harbour.

# Attack Points

You wish to find a cave entrance in a shake, or swallow hole on the other side of a limestone area with nothing more than its grid reference to work on. See Fig. 12.3. Knowing how difficult these depressions are to locate, you simplify the problem by heading to where the scar (a line of limestone outcrop) is intersected by an allotment boundary wall. On reaching this easily discerned position, the map, carefully set by using the marked boundary wall, will point to the depression only a couple of hundred metres or so away. Orienteers, who always seem to have the ability to find the appropriate word, refer to such a place as the junction between scar and wall as an "Attack Point" though again, the technique is as old as navigation itself.

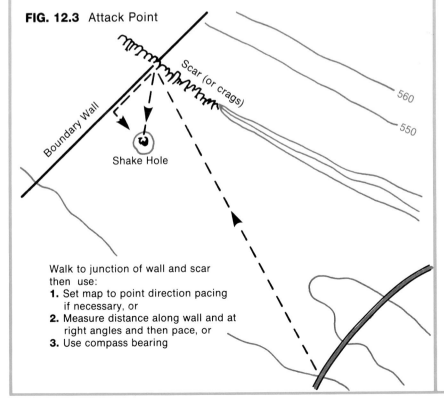

**FIG. 12.3** Attack Point

Boundary Wall

Scar (or crags)

560

550

Shake Hole

Walk to junction of wall and scar then use:
1. Set map to point direction pacing if necessary, or
2. Measure distance along wall and at right angles and then pace, or
3. Use compass bearing

*"In wild country there are fewer landmarks to pinpoint our position".*

## Position Lines

In normal and open country we find our way by using paths and tracking our progress by using landmarks to pinpoint our position. In wild country we tend to rely more on line features such as ridges, edges, spurs and valleys and there are not always as many landmarks in our immediate vicinity to enable us to track our progress. You are following a route on the edge of an escarpment with the valley on your left. See Fig. 12.4. You come abreast of a building A. Because it is a considerable distance away it is difficult, or impossible, to judge when you are directly opposite it. Further on you see two more buildings and as you travel you notice that they eventually become in line. These two places are now said to be "in transit". A line drawn through these two buildings and projected to the ridge along which you are travelling will enable you to fix your position on the ridge with accuracy. Any two point features will do, a stream junction, a knoll or a road junction, so that when you are travelling on higher ground you have a ready means of fixing your position at all times from landmarks some distance away. Line features will also serve the same purpose, a stream or gill on the opposite side of the valley, a road or even a field boundary wall can all be used to provide a position line to fix your position.

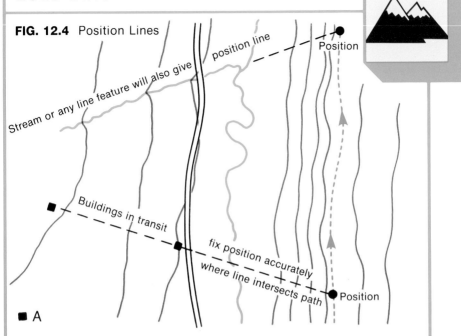

**FIG. 12.4** Position Lines

position line

Stream or any line feature will also give

Position

Buildings in transit

fix position accurately
where line intersects path

Position

A

# Holding a Course Without a Compass

Earlier in this chapter the phrase "travel in the general direction" was used. Experienced hill-walkers and ramblers use this mode of travel as a matter or routine. They head across country in the general direction of their objective and then "home in" on it when it comes into sight. This procedure can be used with surprising accuracy in featureless terrain over very considerable distances, assuming, of course, that visibility is normal. The novice, when confronted with this situation, all too often resorts to the compass for security, and travel becomes painstaking and tedious and certainly not what hill-walking is all about.

You are on the top of Ilkley Moor at the Thimble Stones. See Fig. 12.5. You wish to travel across the moor to the Cow and Calf Rocks but they are out of sight below the level of the moor in Wharfedale. Having set your map and laid your pencil along the line from your position to the Cow and Calf as you would normally do to find your direction of travel, you notice that if the line is continued beyond the rocks, it points to a prominent TV/Radio Mast on the far side of Wharfedale which is clearly visible on the skyline. You can now put your map away for all you have to do is walk in the direction of the

**FIG. 12.5** Holding a course without a compass

Select a landmark beyond objective or a point on the skyline
in the required direction of travel. Head towards this mark
until objective is in sight and then make a visual approach.

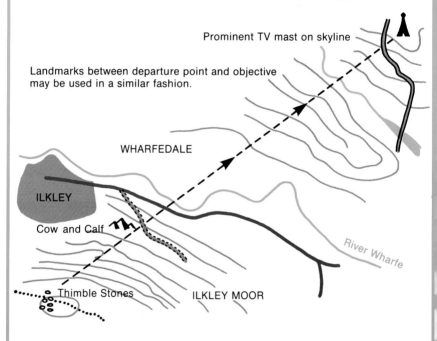

Prominent TV mast on skyline

Landmarks between departure point and objective
may be used in a similar fashion.

WHARFEDALE

ILKLEY

Cow and Calf

River Wharfe

Thimble Stones

ILKLEY MOOR

mast and eventually the rocks will come into view. You do not need to
be able to identify the land mark, it could be a building, a distant peak
or a distinctive part of the skyline; as long as it is in the right direction,
beyond your objective, easily recognisable and not likely to drop out
of sight, it will suffice. If it should drop out of sight select another
mark. If you have to deviate from your course to avoid areas of bog or
marsh it rarely causes any problems. This technique works well on
upland moors and plateaux because they are usually tilted, and on
plains where surrounding hills may make excellent targets.

*"Climbing up gills or gullies provides excellent sport for the scrambler".*

## Gullies and Gills

In the Chapter 'More about Relief', the importance of streams as indicators of direction was stressed and their importance was again emphasized in the chapters dealing with navigation in restricted visibility and "On being lost", especially as a means of finding your way out of the cloud to lower ground. The gills and gullies which have been carved into the steeper flanks of the hills and mountains by the action of water are excellent indicators of direction, but that direction is directly downhill and it can pose a very serious danger to the inexperienced. Climbing up gills or gullies provides excellent sport for the climber and scrambler in both summer and winter with their bare rock, vertical pitches and waterfalls. They are, however, very dangerous places for the hill walker to descend in walking boots and a top heavy backpack, being very wet, slippery and often vertical. Many of our better known waterfalls are to be found in them. Often they are approached on the convex slope on the shoulder of the mountain and it is difficult, at the best of times, to appreciate how

203

steep the slope may become, and it is even worse in cloud or darkness. In spite of the obvious danger they can be a valuable aid in reaching lower ground away from the cloud and the full force of the elements in certain areas of the country, providing you know the terrain and have sufficient experience to be secure on steep slopes. The procedure is never to venture into the gill or gully itself but to follow the shoulder which usually consists of steep grass which can normally be negotiated with care. The locality is all important in deciding whether to follow a gill, for all experienced mountain walkers know of places where the stream disappears over a precipice. If in doubt play safe!

## Streams

Streams are always important factors in mountain and wild country navigation. Like gullies they always lead downhill, and, being line features, they have a geographical direction. On the map they have a dendritic pattern with smaller streams leading into the larger streams like boughs on a tree. Once clear of the steepest slopes they are useful features to follow and valuable in establishing our position. While they are most helpful they do pose problems for the traveller. The smaller ones tend to be unpredictable; disappearing in times of drought and turning into raging torrents in wet weather. In periods of drought they are easily overlooked while in wet weather they can be a serious obstacle to our progress and may enforce long detours. The solution is to anticipate these problems. If the weather is very dry then it is reasonable to assume that the smaller streams may have dried up and special care will be needed in spotting the stream bed. The map itself will give no indication of the size of the stream—the blue lines are usually of the same thickness until they become rivers—so you will have to infer its size from recent rainfall and experience. When descending to the lower ground of a valley in very wet weather it is a wise precaution to ensure that you will be on the correct side of a major stream in flood to enable you to reach your destination. This entails thinking ahead so that you can cross the stream, and any of its tributaries, in the upper reaches where it is still negotiable. If ever you are forced to aim for a collecting feature, such as a road, in bad weather and there is a stream or river between you and it, try and aim for a bridge. There is nothing more frustrating than to be separated by a few metres of water and forced to make a long detour, rather than have to commit oneself or your group to the hazards of a river crossing. It is surprising how many roads run alongside rivers. When following streams in their upper courses it is usually better to keep well clear of the water course itself. Walk alongside the stream some distance away. The terrain near to the stream is usually wet and marshy, frequently boulder-strewn and slippery and always twisting and turning. If there is an existing path beside the stream you will usually see the wisdom of previous walkers. Bear in mind that streams may flow gently in hanging tributary valleys and then suddenly disappear over the edge of a cliff where they meet the main valley. This is most likely to occur in glaciated regions but may occur in any place where the main valley has been eroded more quickly than the tributary valleys. Beware when using streams as an aid to route finding!

*"It is surprising how many roads run alongside rivers".*

SUMMARY

In this chapter, and in previous ones, we have considered all the principal methods of route finding which are available to us using the map alone, and this provides an opportunity to summarize these techniques.

■ Following paths, roads, tracks etc. and tracking progress by using landmarks to pinpoint position. The basic method. Used almost exclusively in normal and greenfield country and extensively used in mountainous and wilderness country.

■ Following linear features such as valleys, spurs, ridges, streams and rivers and tracking progress using landmarks or position lines to pinpoint or fix position. Probably the second most frequently used method of route finding.

■ Selecting a series of landmarks (waymarks) or natural features each of which is visible from the adjacent mark, and which link starting point with destination. A traditional method of pilotage or point to point.

■ Travelling in the general direction of the objective, possibly with the assistance of a landmark beyond the objective, until it is visible and then making a visual approach.

■ Travelling towards a collecting feature and then establishing position on the features to enable a visual approach to be made to the objective.

■ Travelling towards an easily discerned attack point which is nearer to the objective and which will simplify the locating of the objective.

■ Rivers and mountain streams in spate are a formidable obstacle. Think ahead and plan your route with care to avoid being faced with either a long detour or the dangers of a river crossing.

In Chapter 8 we considered the three most vital techniques, with the advice that if you only used the compass infrequently it may be wise to limit your skills to those three. Any confusion which may arise will not occur while reading this book; if it occurs, it will probably be a few years hence on the top of a mountain, in thick cloud with night fall imminent. You alone can decide! Read this chapter, for there are certainly techniques in this chapter which may be of use to you on top of that mountain, and then you can judge whether they will be helpful or just lead to confusion at that vital moment.

Just as it is necessary to entrench the skills of map reading before considering the compass, it will be necessary to entrench the compass skills of Chapter 8 before adding the following skills to your repertoire. If you are prepared to spend the time and effort to master the skills and not let them remain something which you read about in a book, then you should have no trouble.

The modern protractor compass has a marvellous versatility, all the processes which can be carried out with a set map can be performed with the compass, along with many more, the most important of which are listed below. Again it is assumed that the vast majority of use will be in the British Isles or Western Europe where magnetic variation will remain towards the West until well into the next century. The compensation which may be necessary in other parts of the world is dealt with at the end of the chapter; the techniques, of course, remain unchanged. It will be helpful to have your compass and a map to hand while you are considering this chapter.

The most important compass skill—travelling on a bearing—has already been considered. This is the compass equivalent of using the set map to point your direction of travel.

## 1. Geographical Direction

Just as we can use the set map to give geographical direction, in terms of the cardinal and inter-cardinal points, so the compass can be used for orienting. Holding the compass horizontally so that the needle is

**FIG. 13.1** Geographical Direction from the compass

Either rotate the whole compass until red (N) end of
needle is opposite N on the housing
Or turn housing until N is opposite red end of needle

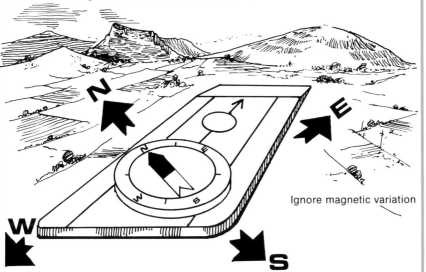

Ignore magnetic variation

swinging freely, turn the compass housing round until the letter "N"
is opposite the red end of the needle. The cardinal and half-cardinal
directions can now be read directly from the compass housing. The
same result can be achieved by turning the whole compass round until
the "N" is opposite the red end of the needle instead of just turning the
housing. There is no need to make any allowance for magnetic
variation when considering general directions such as these. See Fig.
13.1.

## 2. Locating a Feature

Features and landmarks which are marked on the map can be located
in the countryside using the compass instead of the set map. If the
feature is a considerable distance away, or it is a case of locating one
mountain amongst many, then the greater accuracy of the compass
over a set map will be obvious.

(**a**) Find the grid bearing from your location on the map to the feature
on the map by placing the edge of the compass between the two points
with the direction of travel arrow pointing towards the feature. If the
distance between the two points is longer than your compass, lay

209

anything to hand with a straight edge between the two points and place your compass against it. Turn the compass housing round until the orienting lines in the bottom of the housing are parallel with the North/South grid lines on the map and the "N" is pointing to the top of the map. Read off the grid bearing opposite the direction of travel arrow. See Figs. 13.2 and 13.3.

**FIG. 13.2** Locating feature by compass

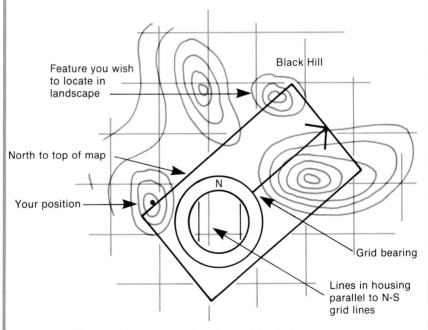

Feature you wish to locate in landscape

Black Hill

North to top of map

Your position

N

Grid bearing

Lines in housing parallel to N-S grid lines

Place compass on your location and the feature.
Turn housing lines until parallel with N-S grid lines on map and N is to top of map – read grid bearing opposite direction arrow.

Add Magnetic Variation
$$\begin{array}{r} 40° \\ +\ 6° \\ \hline 46°\ \text{Magnetic} \end{array}$$

(**b**) Convert the grid bearing to a magnetic bearing. The magnetic variation will differ according to the area you are in and will be found on the map you are using. Because it is to the West in the British Isles it must always be added when working from the map to the country. You will recall the advice of Chapter 8—because the country is always larger than the map, always make the grid bearing larger when

**FIG. 13.3** Locating a feature by compass (Map to country)

Hold the compass in front of you turn round
until the red end of the needle is opposite the N on the
housing and the needle is parallel to the lines in the housing.
The feature lies along this line of sight.

211

working from the map to the country. Using a magnetic variation of 6 degrees West:

Grid bearing                $40°$

Variation                    $+6°$

Magnetic bearing      $46°$ M

Immediately add the variation by turning the housing anti-clockwise for another 6 degrees until the direction of travel arrow is opposite $46°$M.

(**c**) Locate the feature in the countryside. Hold the compass in front of you at about waist level, and horizontally so that the needle is swinging freely. Turn yourself round until the needle is parallel to the orienting lines in the bottom of the housing and the red, or North seeking end of the needle, is against the "N" on the housing. You are now facing towards the feature. Carefully sight along the direction of travel arrow; the feature will lie along that line of sight and you should be able to recognize it. If there are several features of a similar nature then your ability to estimate distance visually will be all important. Make a habit of always noting the distance between you and the feature before you take the bearing. This will not only be of considerable assistance in locating the feature but continually reinforcing your ability to judge distance by the eye. After locating the feature you will be able to say to yourself "That is what 2.5 kilometres looks like", or whatever distance it is. You will have realized by now that the method of locating a feature is exactly the same as travelling on a bearing. The only difference is that we are not going to travel towards the feature.

## 3. Identifying a Feature

This is exactly the opposite procedure to the one above where the intention was to locate and look at some feature found on the map in the countryside. If, on looking around the countryside within your view, you see a landmark or feature, such as mountain or a farm, it can be identified and named by using the compass as an alternative to setting the map.

(**a**) Hold your compass in front of you in the normal manner—waist level and needle swinging freely. Sight the direction of travel arrow

carefully at the feature in question. Then, while taking care not to move the arrow from the feature, turn the compass housing round until the needle is parallel with the orienting lines and the red end against the "N". You can now read off the magnetic bearing of the feature from your position against the direction of travel arrow. See Figs 13.4 and 13.5. Incidentally, if ever you are about to be engulfed in cloud and you can see your objective, or if for a few precious moments the cloud parts to reveal your destination, this is action you

**FIG. 13.4** Identifying a feature (Country to map)

Sight the direction arrow at the feature you wish to identify. Turn the housing until the 'N' is opposite the red end of the needle and the lines in the housing are parallel to the needle – giving the magnetic bearing.

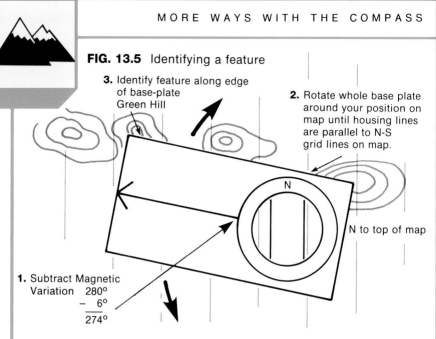

**FIG. 13.5** Identifying a feature

**3.** Identify feature along edge of base-plate Green Hill

**2.** Rotate whole base plate around your position on map until housing lines are parallel to N-S grid lines on map.

N

N to top of map

**1.** Subtract Magnetic Variation  
280°  
−  6°  
274°

should take. Because it is a magnetic bearing you can use it to travel to your objective without further ado; there is no need to ponder on whether to add or subtract variation.

(**b**) Convert the magnetic bearing to a grid bearing. Assuming a magnetic variation of 6 degrees, because the bearing was obtained from the compass needle pointing to the magnetic pole, we need to reduce the bearing by 6 degrees to convert it to a grid bearing which we can use on our map. We can remember this by reasoning that: because the country is larger than the map, we must make the bearings taken from the country smaller when we want to use them on the smaller map. Fig. 13.5. There are a number of memory aids but they can cause confusion, especially if you use your compass in parts of the world where the variation is East.

| | |
|---|---|
| Magnetic bearing | 280° |
| Variation | −6° |
| Grid bearing | 274° |

Immediately subtract the variation by turning the housing clockwise for 6 degrees until 274 is opposite the direction of travel arrow.

(**c**) Identify the feature on the map by placing a long edge of the compass on your position, with the direction of travel arrow pointing away, and then turn the WHOLE compass around until the orienting lines in the bottom of the housing are parallel with a North/South grid line on the map. The feature you wish to identify lies along the line made by the edge of your compass in the direction of the arrow or a projection of that line. By now you will appreciate the advice of never using a compass with a base much less than 10 cm. If your compass will not reach, place a straight edge against your compass. Again the need to be able to estimate distances by the eye cannot be over-stressed. Always estimate the distance of the feature before you take the bearing, and then, after you have found the feature on the map, measure the distance to see how accurate your judgement was.

## 4. Position Lines or Single Back-bearing

In the previous chapter we saw how landmarks which were in transit, or in line, could provide us with a means of locating our position on a line feature such as a path or ridge. A similar technique can be used with the compass. Three conditions should be satisfied:

(**a**) You need to be on a line feature.

(**b**) The landmark in the country must be correctly identified and it must be shown on your map.

(**c**) It should be as near to a right angle as possible to the direction of the line feature.

**4.** (**a**) Take the magnetic bearing of the landmark using the same method as in 3(a). Since you are working from country to map, subtract the magnetic variation to convert it into a grid bearing in the same way as in 3(b). Then place a long edge of your compass on the landmark with the direction of travel arrow pointing away, and then rotate the WHOLE compass until the orienting lines in the bottom of the housing are parallel with a North/South grid line on the map and the S (South) is to the top (North) of the map. Your position is where this line, or a projection of the line, intersects the line feature you are on. Bringing the "S" on the housing to the top, or North of the map produces a back-bearing. This avoids the need to add or subtract 180° from the original bearing. See Fig. 13.6.

215

**FIG. 13.6**  Position Lines (Single back-bearing)

**1.** Take bearing on landmark which is marked on map.
(See "Identifying a Feature"  Figs: 13.4 and 13.5)

**2.** Subtract Magnetic Variation

**3.** Rotate whole base-plate around LANDMARK until housing
lines are parallel to N-S Grid lines and **S** (SOUTH) is to
the TOP (North) of map to give a **back bearing.**

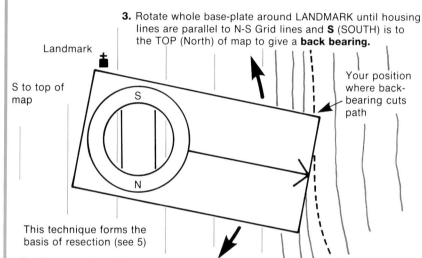

Landmark

S to top of
map

Your position
where back-
bearing cuts
path

This technique forms the
basis of resection (see 5)

## 5. Resection (Establishing position by backbearings)

If, by taking a bearing on a point feature, we can obtain a position
line on which we are located, by taking a second bearing on a different
point we can obtain another position line and the place where these
lines intersect must be our location. We have replaced the line feature
in 4. with a bearing. See Fig. 13.7. I prefer to teach the use of just two
carefully taken bearings as near to a right angle as possible. Sailors by
tradition take three, the lines usually intersecting to form a triangle or
"cocked hat". They place their position in the middle of the triangle
as they may be taking their sightings from a heaving deck. If you
cannot find landmarks at right angles take three bearings, for bearings
at acute and obtuse angles can produce wildly inaccurate results.

Two conditions should be satisfied:

(**a**) There must be two, or possibly three, well separated landmarks.

(**b**) All the landmarks must be positively identified and marked on
your map.

Take bearings on the landmarks and proceed as in 4 but this time plot
the lines from the landmarks on your map using your pencil. Your

**FIG. 13.7** Finding position by resection (Backbearings)

1. Take bearings on two features in landscape, which are marked on map, as near to right angles as possible

2. Subtract magnetic variation (country to map)

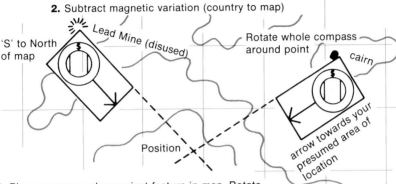

'S' to North of map

Lead Mine (disused)

Rotate whole compass around point

cairn

Position

arrow towards your presumed area of location

3. Place compass edge against feature in map. Rotate whole compass until lines in the housing are parallel with N-S Grid lines on map and the S on the housing is at the top (N) of map to give backbearing. Plot position line. Repeat on other feature. Your position is at the intersection of the lines.

position is at the intersection of the lines. A position which has been established by bearings is a "fix". You have fixed your position as opposed to pinpointing it from adjacent landmarks.

This technique has been the stand-by of many generations of sailors in coastal waters wishing to avoid the hidden shoal or wanting to know if their anchor holds. I am less certain about its use on land, for while I have encountered many who advocate its use, I have found few who have used it "in earnest".

Ordinary hill-walkers finding their way by the map and tracking their position in normal visibility never seem to need it, and when it could be of great use to them in cloud or mist, they cannot see anything on which to take a bearing.

There is one situation when it could be of some value—when a member of a party is injured or suffering from hypothermia and a couple are setting off to fetch help, and the visibility is good. If the incident occurs well away from landmarks which would enable you to pinpoint your position, in the middle of featureless terrain, then two or three bearings would establish your position. This fix could be of great help to the rescue team who may only reach the area in the dark

217

or after the cloud has covered the scene. The position should be plotted on the map and the particular map should be carried by those fetching help.

Resection may help to establish your location when you have descended out of the cloud on higher ground and you are completely lost. You have obviously come down the wrong spur or valley and you are utilizing your procedure for being lost. All the terrain above you will be in cloud so you will have to find landmarks below you to fix your position. The problem is—are you able to positively identify two or three landmarks on which to take bearings? To take a bearing on an incorrectly identified landmark makes matters worse. If you can correctly identify two or three landmarks are you still lost? However, if you are able to identify two or three point features with certainty, take bearings and fix your position. This will either establish your position or confirm it, which is very reassuring after you have been lost. Then work out a fresh route to your destination.

*"Resection may help to establish your location when you descend out of cloud".*

## 6. Checking Your Route or Position by a Backbearing

If you are travelling in a featureless area using the compass in the normal manner and you feel that you may have strayed off course—"side-slipped", providing you can see your starting point, or a positively identified position on your route, it is very simple to check if you are off course. Turn round holding the compass in the usual way until the white end (South seeking end) is opposite the "N". You are now facing in exactly the opposite direction. If you sight along the direction of travel arrow then your departure point should be on that line. If it is not move to your left or right until it is in line when you take a sight. See Fig. 13.8. There is no need to think about magnetic variation because you have already taken care of that before you set out. This is a very useful technique; with a little imagination and practice it can be used in all kinds of situations to check your whereabouts.

**FIG. 13.8** Checking route by backbearing

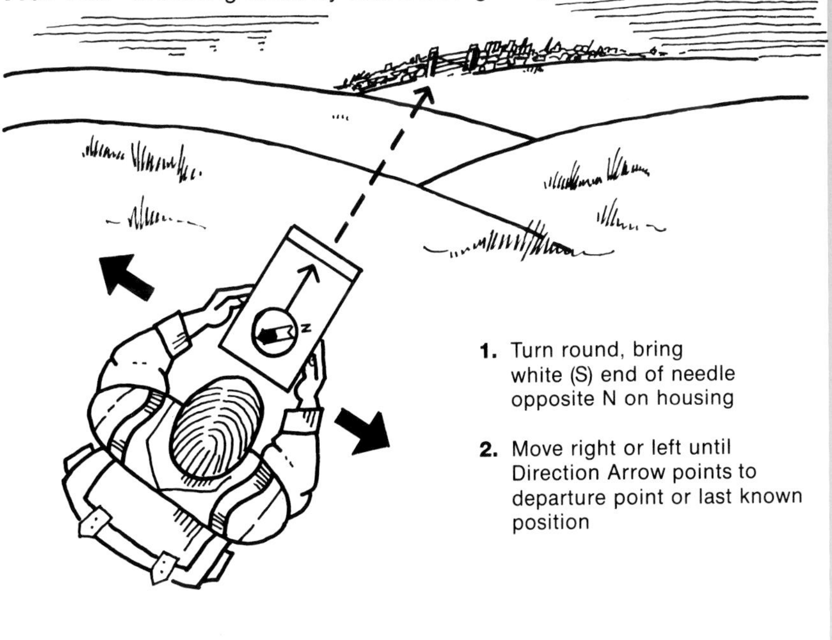

1. Turn round, bring white (S) end of needle opposite N on housing

2. Move right or left until Direction Arrow points to departure point or last known position

## 7. Aiming Off

This is a simple technique. You are at a sheep-fold X, see Fig. 13.9, and you wish to travel to the footbridge over the river at Y, where your vehicle is parked by the road. The weather is bad with visibility around 100 metres and night is fast approaching. If you plot a course directly to the bridge you think you may well miss it in the prevailing conditions, as it is over 2 km away. You will not know whether to turn up or downstream to find it. Rather than waste time in the bad weather searching, you deliberately aim off 10 degrees upstream. Upstream is slightly nearer than aiming 10 degrees downstream so it will shorten the distance. You know that you can normally hold a course to within 5 degrees so you feel you have an ample margin for error. Work out the magnetic bearing in the usual way and then subtract 10 degrees to take you to the North. (If it was more convenient to head downstream then you would need to add 10 degrees.) Walk on the bearing in the usual way until you reach the river and then turn and travel downstream until you reach the bridge.

**FIG. 13.9** Aiming Off

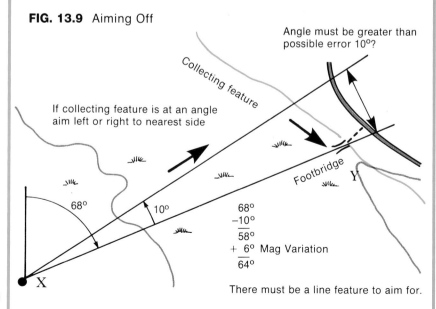

Angle must be greater than possible error 10°?

If collecting feature is at an angle aim left or right to nearest side

Collecting feature

Footbridge

68°

10°

68°
−10°
‾‾‾‾
58°
+ 6° Mag Variation
‾‾‾‾
64°

X

Y

There must be a line feature to aim for.

Aiming-off is a very old technique and the nineteenth century sailor utilized a very elegant variation to enable him to locate isolated ocean islands. He would aim off sufficiently far to one side or the other of his destination to be certain as to whether it would lie to port or starboard. By taking an observation on a heavenly body during morning twilight, or on the sun at, or after, sunrise he would be able to obtain a position line at right angles to the azimuth, or direction, of the heavenly body. Using his tables, this position line would then be plotted on the chart, where it could be carried forward by dead reckoning, for use later in the day. When this position line intercepted his objective he would turn to port or starboard and "run down the position line" to his destination.

This technique will only work for you if there is a collecting feature to head for. If in Fig. 13.9 you were trying to reach the sheep fold from the bridge in the same weather conditions then this method would only make the situation worse. Not only would you miss your objective but you would not know when to turn, and it is nearly always harder to estimate distance travelled than direction. If you wished to reach the sheep-fold in bad visibility use the following technique.

## 8. Dead Reckoning

If you wish to travel to a point feature, such as a bothy in the middle of a moor, in restricted visibility and there is no attack point, or if you are already at the attack point, there is no alternative but to head directly for your target and rely on your ability with the compass and to judge distance. Work out the magnetic bearing of the objective and then measure the distance between it and your departure point. Take special care with both the bearing and the distance, for there will be no opportunity to remedy careless work after you have committed yourself to the course. Estimating the distance travelled in situations such as this is usually more difficult than holding the course.

(**a**) If it is a matter of some hundreds of metres away then calculate, or use your measure, to find out how many paces will be required to reach it. If you are in a party, delegate one to count the paces (use pebbles or coins like cricket umpires as a tally for each hundred paces) while you walk in the lead with the compass. If you are by yourself you will have to do both. If you hit the bothy all well and good, your reward for excellent compass work. If not commence a square search at the end of the paced distance (**10**) or a sweep search a short distance before you expect to reach your target (**9**).

(**b**) If the objective is more than some hundreds of metres away then, rather than attempting to count paces, you will have to rely on your ability to estimate the distance travelled from the time you have been travelling.

Speed of travel × time = distance travelled

The only guide to your speed of travel is previous experience; hence the emphasis throughout the book on timing travel. Make a conscious effort to find out how long it takes to travel a kilometre and 100 metres of different types of terrain such as footpath, ordinary grassland, rough moor, cotton-grass, grit moor or woodland.

Work out the time to cover a kilometre and then divide to get the time over 100 metres. If you can only find a few hundred metres of suitable forest or woodland, simple proportion will provide the answers, but the greater the distances involved the more reliable your answers will be. Make a note of the these times and carry them with you.

After measuring the distance, calculate the time required to cover the distance. Before setting off make a careful note of the time or start your stop watch. If you are in a party delegate someone to keep check of the time while you concentrate on the compass. If you do not reach your objective at the end of the estimated time commence a square search (**10**) or a sweep search (**9**). This technique is a corner-stone of classical navigation. Pilots in the First World War referred to this method of navigation as flying by "watch and compass" and we can still apply the same phrase when we use it.

## 9. Sweep Search

A rescue team has been called out to retrieve a casualty suffering from hypothermia. The persons who went to seek assistance know that the casualty and companions are sheltering in a ruined shooting box on the moor. Cloud is down on the moor and it is dusk with visibility around 100 or 150 metres. A course is plotted from the nearest attack point to the shooting box, just over 2 kilometres away. The dead reckoning method is used, travelling on a bearing and using travelled time to determine the distance covered. The time of departure is noted and the team set out. A little while before the estimated time to reach the shooting box has elapsed the party should stop and note the time, and then spread out in a line. Members should be spaced at a distance just under the limit of visibility, with the navigator in the middle and just ahead of the line. After noting the time the party should then proceed. See Fig. 13.10. Using this method a party of eight could

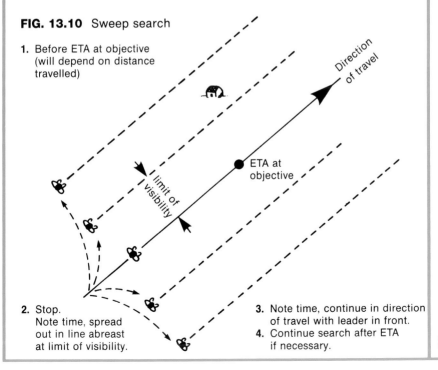

**FIG. 13.10** Sweep search

1. Before ETA at objective (will depend on distance travelled)

*Direction of travel*

ETA at objective

*limit of visibility*

2. Stop.
   Note time, spread out in line abreast at limit of visibility.

3. Note time, continue in direction of travel with leader in front.
4. Continue search after ETA if necessary.

223

sweep a path about a kilometre wide in visibility of between 100 and 150 metres and they should have no problems at all in locating the shooting box after following a bearing for just over 2 kilometres. A small group of hill-walkers can extend their range of sight very considerably by using this method; with visibility around 100 metres a party of four can extend their range of sight to nearly half a kilometre, more than enough to cover most errors in the use of the compass. More importantly it helps to overcome the problem of estimating distance. When navigating by dead reckoning the use of this technique should always be considered.

The sweep search is one of the most widely used methods of finding people, or objects, and it is particularly useful in searching steep-sided valleys or spurs though it can be utilized elsewhere. In valleys and on spurs it has the advantage of being less tiring for the searchers, poses few navigational problems and is fairly easy to control. The search should take place "along the feature". The team is spaced out according to the nature of the terrain, the prevailing visibility and how conspicuous the object of the search is. The leader, or navigator, should always take the edge of the sweep along which the return sweep will be made so that there is no danger of an area being left unsearched. Markers are most useful in defining the area searched. See Fig. 13.11.

## 10. Square Search

The square search is a much more sophisticated technique than the sweep search. It was devised to cope with the problems of searching an area of sea but it now forms the basis of air searches as well. Since it is virtually impossible to navigate a ship or an aircraft on a circular path in an ever expanding spiral, the technique involves travelling on a series of legs at right angles to each other.

In spite of its apparent sophistication, the square search is not difficult to use and well within the capability of average hill-walkers; occasionally it may prove to be the only practical solution to their problems. Its main purpose is to search an area of featureless terrain, or locate an object in restricted visibility—AROUND A KNOWN OR PRESUMED LOCATION. It is an excellent method for an individual, a small group or even a small rescue team to use, but the

224

**FIG. 13.11.** Sweep search

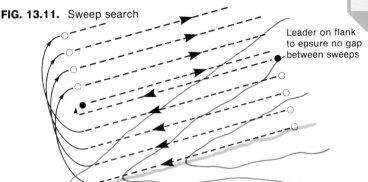

Leader on flank to ensure no gap between sweeps

Sweep along feature – valley, ridge.
Searchers spaced according to visibility or size of object of search-injured person, crashed aircraft.
Use line features for boundaries where possible or flour which will not damage environment.

mind boggles at the thought of controlling a large party. It is the only practical method for the individual to locate a shelter on a plateau or moor in cloud or in darkness. A small group would have to use this method if they failed to locate their objective by spreading out in a line. A small search party on reaching the presumed locality of a casualty in featureless terrain would probably find this the best solution.

A small group fails to locate a bothy on a plateau at the end of the estimated time while walking on a bearing in poor visibility. On reaching the presumed location, the group should stop and check the visibility distance. (A person walks away until almost out of sight and then turns and paces the distance back). See Fig. 13.12. Set the letter "N" on the compass against the direction of travel arrow and then walk in the direction of Magnetic North for a distance equal to the limit of visibility, with someone pacing the distance. This is one unit of distance. Stop, turn round until the compass needle is pointing to the letter "W" on the compass housing and then walk for two units of distance, or twice the distance of visibility. Stop, turn to the South and then walk for three units. Keep increasing the distance by one unit at each turn until the objective is located. You may start in a different direction, but always use a cardinal point, or go the other way around in an anti-clockwise direction but it is vital to avoid confusion.

225

**FIG. 13.12** Square search

Must be around a presumed location or ETA.
Determine distance of visibility if necessary (56 double paces).
Reduce to round figure 50 paces = 1 unit of distance.
Search on Cardinal points (magnetic) N to Direction of travel arrow.
Red end of needle to N.W.S.E for clockwise search.
N.E.S.W for anti-clockwise.

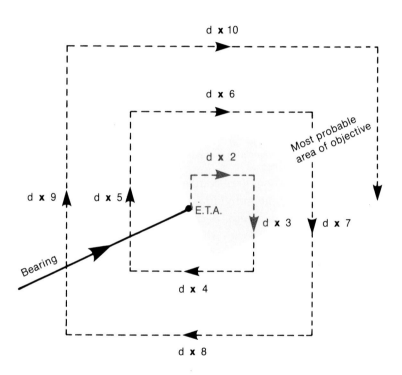

Your objective will most probably be ahead or to your left or right.
There is advantage in searching this area first. The initial choice
of direction can assist this. If you go to your left, search clockwise
if to your right, search anti-clockwise. This can be done whatever
the original direction of travel.

## 11. Right Angled Deviation

The same compass technique used in the square search can be used to
move round obstacles when travelling in restricted visibility or
featureless terrain. If while travelling on a bearing you are confronted
with an obstacle such as a swamp and you can see the other side, the
obvious solution is to identify a clump of sedge on the far side and then

**FIG. 13.13** Right angled deviation

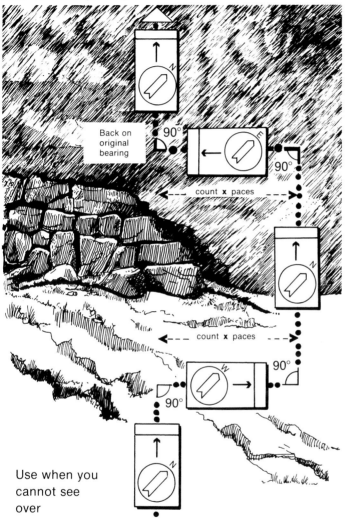

Back on original bearing

90°

count **x** paces

90°

90°

count **x** paces

90°

90°

Use when you cannot see over

walk round to the mark and then carry on; a couple of metres one side or the other will make little difference. If you cannot see over the obstacle—a rock outcrop, a clump of trees—the following method should be used. Decide which is the best way round. If right, turn in the preferred direction until the red, or North, end of the needle is opposite the "W" on the housing, see Fig. 12.10. Travel in the direction indicated counting the number of double paces until you have cleared

227

the obstruction. Stop and return to your original course by turning until the needle is back to "N". Walk until you have cleared the obstacle—there is no need to count paces as you are travelling on your original bearing unless you were using pacing as a method of determining distance originally. Stop and turn in the opposite direction to your first deviation until the red end of the needle is opposite the "E" and then count the same number of double paces to return you to your original line of travel. If you wish to go left-about round the obstacle bring the needle to "E" first. There is obviously no need to bother with magnetic variation or make any alterations to the compass setting.

## 12. Direction of Slope

In Chapter 6 on 'More about Relief', the importance of "up" and "down" as directional aids was discussed; how "up" was significant in enabling walkers and climbers to reach their objective while "down" frequently posed problems and accounted for most people getting lost during the descent. While the orientation of spurs and valleys is widely used as an aid to direction, sufficient attention is not always paid to the direction of the slopes which form the flanks of mountains and hills.

If in Fig. 13.14 you were facing directly down the hill and you knew the direction of the slope was due West, you could only be in one place on the hill—you must be located on a position line running due West from the summit. Though this is a simplistic example, the principle forms the basis of a valuable aid to both direction and location in restricted visibility. Even when visibility is restricted it is usually possible to determine the direction of maximum gradient; it may be the only direction we can appreciate. This direction then determines the direction the slope is facing.

Move to one side, if necessary, to ensure that you have a true representation of the slope, though a gully may serve, and take a bearing directly down the slope in exactly the same way as if you were taking a bearing on a landmark. Subtract the variation (country to map) and you now have the direction of the slope. On a hill of simple

**FIG. 13.14** Slope direction

On a hill of simple shape if you were facing west directly downhill you could only be on one position line.

outline this alone will establish your general position and prevent the novice from heading down the wrong side. To obtain a position line place the compass in the presumed area of the slope. Turn the whole compass until the orienting lines in the bottom of the housing are parallel with the North/South grid lines on the map with the "N" towards the North of the map, and the direction of travel arrow pointing down the slope. Move the compass around the slope until the edge of the compass crosses the contours at right angles. You will soon acquire the ability to move the compass around the map keeping the orienting lines in the housing parallel to the grid lines as you change from one grid line to another. You are located on the position line where the edge of the compass crosses the contours at right angles. This technique can be of considerable help in restricted visibility. It may not always enable those who are lost to establish their location, but at least it may assist in establishing the area of probability. See Fig. 13.15. Even on a mountain of fairly complex outline, with valleys and spurs, it is surprising how few slopes have the same direction and this method can at least help to narrow down your location to one or two places. Get the map and compass out one evening and carry out a few experiments in the comfort of an armchair.

**FIG. 13.15** Slope direction

1. Use compass to determine the direction of the steepest gradient
2. Subtract Magnetic Variation (ground to map)

orienting lines parallel to grid lines

775

750

contours at right angles

pointing downhill

move whole compass

3. Move whole compass around presumed slope with orienting lines in housing parallel to N-S grid lines with direction arrow pointing downhill until contours are perpendicular to edge of compass

## 13. Chain Walking

During the daylight hours cloud or fog rarely reduces visibility to below 50 or 100 metres which is quite sufficient for the normal sighting technique to be used and, with experience, it is possible to travel reasonably quickly and confidently. Similarly at night it is nearly always possible to use this method, or more frequently sight on a more distant feature or the skyline. When darkness and thick fog combine you may be compelled to chain walk, while in blizzard or white-out conditions it may be the only way to move at all. If this technique is to be used it should be practised beforehand. The top of a mountain, in a howling snow-storm with white-out conditions, when you cannot even see your own feet, is not the best place either to teach or learn this technique, as I found out the hard way in the middle of a February night while searching for a crashed fighter plane.

The usual technique taught in military manuals is as follows:

The magnetic bearing is worked out in the usual way. The navigator stands still and sends a person ahead to the limit of visibility in the general direction of travel. He then directs the person who has gone ahead to move to right or left until the person is on the precise course. Directing the person is done by word of mouth. If silence is required, the navigator estimates how far off course the person is and then

**FIG. 13.16** Chain Walking

**1.** Walk to limit of visibility on compass bearing

**2.** Turn and bring white (S) end of needle to N on housing (giving back bearing)
**3.** Move left or right until Direction Arrow points at group
**4.** Bring up group and repeat.

moves to what is assumed to be the correct position with the rest of party. See Fig. 13.16. This method can be very tedious and time consuming. Though hill-walkers can shout directions, it is exhausting and often it is difficult to hear above the roar of the wind. I confess to being totally perplexed by diagrams where lines of people keep leap-frogging around each other, and can only silently admire the leader who can control such manoeuvres in a force eight wind with visibility down to 50 metres.

231

I suggest that you use the following method:

Work out the compass bearing in the usual way.

Tell the party to remain stationary.

Hold the compass in the usual way and move in the direction indicated by the direction of travel arrow, glancing back, until you reach the limit of visibility. Turn round and bring the white, or South seeking end of the compass needle opposite the "N". You now have a back bearing. Sight in the usual manner and then move to right or left until you are on course. At night a person may point a torch towards the ground to assist you. Bring the rest of the party up to you, and then repeat the process. If pacing is required this should be delegated. The method is simple, quick and effective. No one has to be directed, which is the time-consuming element in the traditional method, and there is no need to shout above the wind telling someone to stop or move to left or right. The leader or navigator, presumed to be the most experienced, is out in front and in a better position to judge the terrain and how far to travel. See Fig. 13.17.

Try and avoid chain walking if you can. You can never travel at more than half the speed attained by using the compass in the normal way. There are usually satisfactory alternatives except in the very worst visibility. When travelling over snow or sand in good visibility remember that your tracks will always show if you are holding course, in the same way as the wake of a ship or boat gives direction.

**FIG. 13.17** Chain walking. Traditional Method.
Person moves to limited visibility in pointed direction.
Then moves left or right on directions, or signals, from navigator until in line with direction of travel.

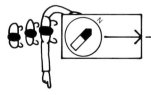

or the navigator judges how much the person is to the left or right of the direction of travel and then moves up to the assumed correct position.

# Errors in Using the Compass

The limiting factor in the use of the protractor type compass is the ability to sight accurately. Its advantages far outweigh this limitation for the vast majority of users. With practice, a very high level of accuracy can be obtained and the limitation tends to rest with the user rather than the instrument. No compass is perfect, however, and each compass has its own Individual Compass Error or ICE, though it is usually not worth taking into account with this type of compass. ICE varies with direction and ship and aircraft compasses have to be calibrated individually. While the limitations of the protractor compass make it unnecessary to bother about the difference between True and Grid North, magnetic variation should not be ignored when taking bearings or walking on a bearing. Take a place in Northern Ireland where the magnetic variation is 9 degrees West. If the variation is ignored, after travelling for 1 kilometre on a bearing you would be 156 metres off course. See Fig. 13.18. If the visibility was

**FIG. 13.18** Errors in using the compass. (Not to scale)

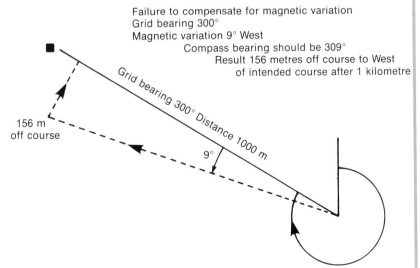

Failure to compensate for magnetic variation
Grid bearing 300°
Magnetic variation 9° West
Compass bearing should be 309°
Result 156 metres off course to West
of intended course after 1 kilometre

Grid bearing 300° Distance 1000 m

9°

156 m
off course

**FIG. 13.19** Errors in using the compass.

To obtain distance off course for any angle of deviation from the intended course:
Multiply distance travelled by the sine of the angle of deviation

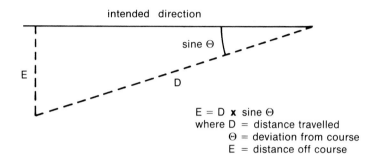

intended direction

sine $\Theta$

E

D

$E = D \times \sin \Theta$
where $D$ = distance travelled
$\Theta$ = deviation from course
$E$ = distance off course

down to between 50 and 100 metres you would not see your objective as you passed it. It is possible to work out how far you would be off course for any particular angle of variation by multiplying the distance travelled by the sine of the angle. See Fig. 13.19.

You should be able to travel on a bearing and be within 5 degrees of your objective. Similarly you should be able to take bearings and be accurate to within 5 degrees. You should practise until you can achieve this standard of proficiency. To expect more of the protractor type compass would be unreasonable but this level of accuracy is more than sufficient for our everyday needs. If you wish to be more accurate you will have to use either a prismatic or a sighting compass, preferably one which has been calibrated.

If you should ever try to fix your position by resection you should bear in mind the limitations of your compass. Bearings on peaks 12 kilometres away (not far in terms of mountain vision) and at right angles to each other would only establish your position to within 4 square kilometres, which again brings into question the value of resection. To establish your position with certainty the landmarks on which you sight must be reasonably near and in such a situation you may be able to pinpoint your position.

*"The weather can affect speed of travel as much as the nature of the terrain".*

Not all the problems in compass navigation arise from the compass itself. If you can achieve an accuracy of around 5 degrees most of your problems in restricted visibility will probably be due to estimating distance incorrectly. There is always a strong tendency to over-estimate the distance travelled in bad visibility. It is important that you practise estimating distance and pacing so that this aspect does not detract from your skill with the compass. On a level path you will be able to measure distance to within a few metres but on the hill with so many different factors to take into account—the surface, fatigue, load, the slope, the stops to use the compass, you will probably only achieve an accuracy of around 10%.

When you are estimating the distance travelled from the time you have been travelling in good visibility, which is always good practice, you should endeavour to be accurate to within 10 or 15%. In restricted visibility while using the compass, and when you are most in need of this ability, your accuracy may well drop to only 20 or 25%.

235

SUMMARY

All the techniques which can be used with a set map can be carried out with the compass. The compass may be regarded as a bridge between the map and the country.

Using the set map to point direction becomes "travelling on a bearing".

Instead of using the map to pinpoint position, we can fix our position by resection or back bearings.

It is possible to locate and identify features and landmarks by compass bearings. In addition to these techniques, there are many others which will cover practically all eventualities to be encountered on land. Some involve adding the magnetic variation while in others the variation has to be subtracted. It is essential that the skills are practised to avoid the possibility of confusion.

# CHAPTER 14

# DIRECTION FROM
# NATURAL PHENOMENA

Nature is full of direction indicators besides the more obvious ones such as the sun, moon and stars. For the person who is interested, and enjoys the natural world, they can provide endless fascination. The problem is that to understand their subtlety and read their message you need to be a very proficient navigator already. You will become more proficient at finding your way by studying your map and compass than by studying where the moss grows on trees.

To make the most effective use of your time confine your attention to the sun, moon and stars and give a little attention to the direction of the wind. Your direction should always come from—the country, your map and the compass. Look up on natural phenomena as aids to navigation not as a means of navigation. Always remember that they will most likely be absent or obscured by cloud when you need them most. If you bear these points in mind you will find that they can be of considerable assistance to you in everyday, and night, route finding, and frequently provide that hint of warning when all is not going to plan.

## Sun

The sun rises towards the East and sets roughly in the West. Twice a year it rises due East and sets due West. At noon (Greenwich Mean Time—GMT—in the UK) it is due South. Depending on your longitude within your time zone you can rely on it being within about five degrees of True South at noon. It moves 15 degrees towards the West each hour but in the plane of the ecliptic, not the horizon. There is a method of finding the approximate North/South line by the use of a watch—assuming that your watch is not digital. Because the apparent movement of the sun is so complex the method can have an error of up to 25 degrees even when you ignore the difficulty of sighting along the hour hand of your watch. This method must surely date from the time of the pocket watch, when every properly dressed explorer carried his gold hunter. The technique is in the Appendices, but it is far easier to carry your compass.

The most effective way to use the sun is to orient the sun and then let the sun orient you, in the same way that you orient the landscape before you start to travel. When you are setting the landscape before you move from your place of departure or checkpoint also make a note of the direction of the sun. Note the relationship between the sun's direction and your intended direction of travel; it is quite adequate to use the cardinal and half-cardinal points. Do this at every checkpoint. Gradually you will form the habit of relating your direction of travel to it, and if the sun suddenly appears to be in the wrong place a little alarm bell will ring and tell you to check your direction of travel. The sun will, of course, be gradually changing direction; in three hours it will change about 45 degrees, say from South-East to South, but you will learn to make this adjustment. Used in this way the sun becomes the best of nature's direction markers. During your journeys in the outdoors try and find out more about the sun's movements, where it rises in winter, or where it sets in summer. Even after it has set the sun can provide direction from the "after-glow" which can persist for a long time in summer nights. Similarly there is a lightening of the sky towards the East before dawn.

## Moon

The movements of the moon are even more complex to understand than those of the sun. The moon's greatest contribution to route finding is that it provides light at night. The amount of light may seem insignificant when compared with the sun, but it is of tremendous value. The amount of light, even that provided by a new or old moon, is rarely appreciated by city dwellers with their street lighting. The moon should be used in the same way as the sun—find its direction and then use it to give direction to you. Do this before the start of each leg and you will learn to relate it to your direction of travel in the same way that you would use the sun.

## Stars

The pole star, Polaris, is the most accurate of nature's directional aids, being situated almost directly over the earth's axis of rotation. To be precise it is never more than 2 degrees away from True North in our latitudes. It is easily located from the pointer stars in the constellation of Ursa Major or the Great Bear, or the Plough, or Jack and his Waggon, or the Big Dipper. The distinctive "W" of Cassiopeia on the other side of Polaris to the Plough is also a guide. See Fig. 14.1.

The rest of the stars appear to rotate round the Pole Star and do not provide direction for us by themselves, but the ones near to the horizon are excellent points to aim for when travelling at night. Using your compass, select a star which appears over your direction of travel,

**FIG. 14.1** Finding the Pole Star.

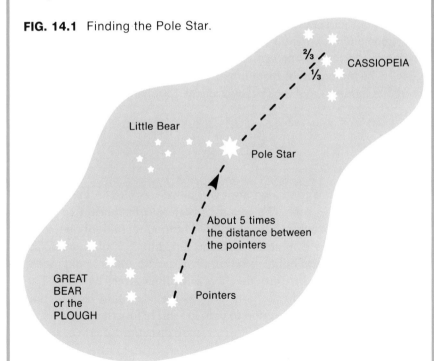

carefully note its relation to the other stars around it so that you will not mistake its identity and then walk towards it. Over the course of an hour it will change direction by under 15 degrees in relation to the horizon (15 degrees in the plane of the ecliptic), so after about twenty minutes you may need to stop and get out your compass and select another star over your direction of travel. Repeat the change every twenty minutes if necessary. See Fig. 14.2. You will be deflected by the star's movement towards the West but this error is of little significance when using a protractor type compass; but if you do not know which of two stars to aim at choose the more easterly. The method can be used equally well when not using the compass, such as when you are travelling in the general direction of a place or towards a collecting feature.

**FIG. 14.2** Apparent movement of the stars.

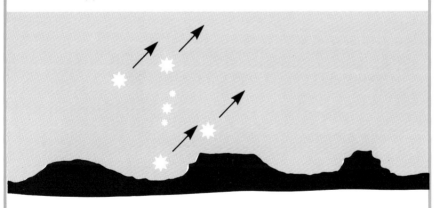

Stars near the horizon rise in the East and set in the West, except at the Poles where they circle round.
Apparent movement depends on latitude and the direction of the horizon you are facing.
Choose an easily distinguished star to avoid confusion because you will not be able to keep your eyes on it all the time.

*"The relationship between the sun and your direction of travel"*.

## Wind

The wind can be used like the sun, moon and stars as a direction marker. The prevailing wind in the British Isles is from the West but it blows from all directions and changes over a period of time. It also funnels up and down valleys and over cols, deflected by hills and mountains and eddies on the lee sides. In spite of all these inconsistencies, when used with understanding it is of considerable value. Though the wind does change direction it is unlikely to change much over the time taken to travel a leg of your journey, probably no more than the direction of the sun or stars. By noting the direction of the wind at the same times as you set your map and the country you have an additional marker. It has the doubtful advantage that you can actually feel it, and it can be most effective in warning you of any unintentional changes of direction.

Those who find their way by the map will probably have more need of the assistance of the sun, stars, moon and the wind than those who perpetually follow their compass needle, but their reward will be that they will see a great deal more and have a greater awareness and appreciation of their presence.

*"The prevailing westerly wind has a significant effect on the vegetation".*

## SUMMARY

The sun, moon, stars and wind are the most useful natural aids to direction. They should be used in conjunction with the map and compass. The most effective way of using them is to orient them so that they can orient you—feed direction into them so that they can provide you with direction later on.

Though they change their direction, it is a comparatively slow change and, in the case of sun, moon and stars, it is predictable.

The wind, though less predictable, is still a valuable aid to direction and, like the others, can alert you very quickly to changes in your direction of travel.

Stars near to the horizon are excellent markers to sight on when using the compass at night.

# CHAPTER 15

# USING YOUR MAP
# AND COMPASS ABROAD

The techniques of map and compass remain the same wherever you are, though the emphasis may change considerably between one technique and another and some minor modifications are sometimes necessary to the techniques themselves. Only in polar regions does it become necessary to call on the techniques of the professional navigator and the equipment at his disposal.

## Compass

The first significant difference in using the compass is that the magnetic variation may not be to the West as in the British Isles, and the variation may change quite significantly over shorter distances. It may be necessary to be on the look-out for more significant local magnetic anomalies. In Western Europe the magnetic variation decreases as you move into Central Europe and then changes to an easterly variation. In the Alps for example, the variation is less than the difference between Grid North and True North on the Norfolk coast. Like the difference between True and Grid North, variation of around two or three degrees can be ignored when using the orienteering compass. In these areas the map bearing is the same as the compass bearing and the process is more simple than in the British Isles.

In other parts of the world you will have to adjust your method to either easterly or westerly variation and there is the old sailor's rhyme to assist you:

Compass West, compass best;
Compass East, compass least.

In other words when the variation is West the bearing must be made better—increased. When the variation is to the East the variation must be lowered—decreased. See Fig. 15.1.

In an area where the variation is to the East all the processes are reversed. When working from map to country the variation is subtracted, while when working from the country to the map, when you are taking bearings on landmarks, you have to add the variation. It is rather like having to drive on the other side of the road in a

**FIG. 15.1** Magnetic Variation East and West

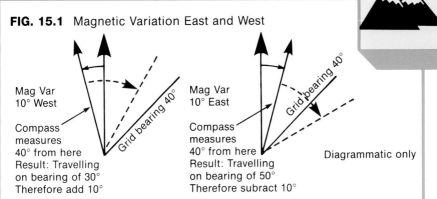

Mag Var
10° West

Compass
measures
40° from here
Result: Travelling
on bearing of 30°
Therefore add 10°

Mag Var
10° East

Compass
measures
40° from here
Result: Travelling
on bearing of 50°
Therefore subtract 10°

Diagrammatic only

foreign country; you need to remember to change back again when you return to these islands.

Another difference you may have to cope with is the absence of grid lines on the maps of many countries. Some maps have no grid lines, only the lines of latitude and longitude. Since a line of longitude is a great circle through the poles, they point to True North but they are rarely conveniently placed for the orienting lines in the bottom of your compass housing. You will have to draw your own, using a sharp pencil, parallel to a line of longitude. There may be divisions on the top and bottom of the map to help you. Do this indoors before your departure for the problems of doing it out of doors in the wind, rain or snow are considerable.

# Maps

Most of Western Europe is surveyed at the 1:50000 scale, with some countries having larger scales in addition. The quality of the mapping and of the finished map varies a little but the general standard is high. In addition to the possible absence of grid lines, many maps show their military origins by the use of mils instead of degrees as a means of angular measurement. All NATO land forces use mils for angular measurement, though naval and air forces continue to use degrees. There are 6400 mils in a circle; 1600 mils in a right angle. North is zero and direction is measured in the normal clockwise direction. The symbol is an "m" with an oblique line through it. See Fig. 15.2. One degree is equal to 18 mils. Once you have worked out the magnetic variation, in the unlikely event of it not being given in degrees as well, continue to use degrees in the usual way.

247

**FIG. 15.2** Mils

Mil = m̗ or 1600

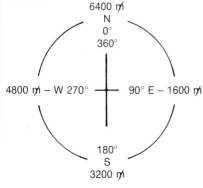

17.8 m̗ = 1 degree
1 m̗ = 3.4 minutes

**FIG. 15.3** Grade

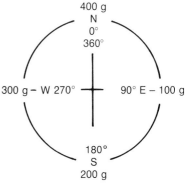

1 grade = 100 centigrades
1 grade = 54 minutes
– Decimalized right angle –

Some foreign maps—such as German and Swiss, also use the Grade method of angular measurement, what might be termed a decimalized right angle. Each right angle or quadrant is divided into 100 grades so there are 400 grades in the circle. Each grade can be subdivided into 100 centigrades in the same way that a degree can be subdivided into minutes and seconds of arc. See Fig. 15.3.

Projections other than the Transverse Mercator used for Ordnance Survey maps are used on foreign maps. This will not create any problems but beware, when plotting a bearing, of assuming that the left and right hand edges of the map run North/South. Check for the divergence of the lines of longitude and use those.

Pay careful attention to the contour or vertical interval of the map and notice if it changes with altitude.

It is possible to purchase foreign maps in this country, and a wide range of Western European maps of the more popular areas may be available off the shelf.

France, the first country in the world to undertake a national survey, did so in the 18th century using the Cassini projection. It is well mapped, as one would expect, and topographical maps are available at both the 1:50000 and 1:25000 scale.

*Reproduced with the permission of the Swiss Federal Office of Topography from March 7th 1989.*

German maps have a familiar look about them and the whole country is covered by 1:50000 maps. A 1:25000 example is shown opposite.

Switzerland produces beautiful maps at both the 1:50000 and 1:25000 scale with fine representation of the rock and ice in the mountainous areas.

All the other countries of Western Europe are covered at a scale of 1:50000, though the mountainous areas of Norway are only covered at the 1:100000 scale. The Republic of Ireland is covered at a scale of one inch to one mile or 1:63360.

There is a book *World Mapping Today*, which may be helpful in obtaining maps for expeditions in more distant places. It is expensive and so it is only likely to be found in major or academic libraries, but your local library may be able to obtain it on the inter-loan system. It covers the whole world and indexes all the maps currently available at their different scales along with the names and addresses of their producers.

## The Altimeter

While the altimeter may be regarded as a luxury in the British Isles its use may be more of a necessity in some parts of the world where, with peaks of far greater height, ridges, spurs and glaciers many kilometres long and the very vastness of slopes posing serious problems of location at the best of times, the vertical dimension takes on much greater significance in relation to horizontal distance. This factor, coupled with the probability of a total absence of man-made landmarks, creates difficulties which are greatly exacerbated by bad visibility. Any instrument which will give assistance in such situations is a most valuable aid, especially if the navigator has a responsibility to others. The altimeter is simply a small pocket-sized aneroid barometer and as such it measures the air pressure, or the weight of the column of air above it. The pressure decreases as you ascend and increases as you descend; the altimeter is calibrated in metres or feet so that the altitude may be read directly off the scale. It is important to choose an

250

*Amtliche Sonderkarte. Karte 1 : 25000 Holsteinische Schweiz.*
*Vervielfältigt mit Genehmigung des Landesvermessungsamtes*
*Schleswig-Holstein vom 13.01.89, 3-562.6, S 69/89.*

251

instrument which is compatible with the units of altitude used on the maps in the principal areas of use. In Britain and Europe a calibration in metres would be the obvious choice. An altimeter will weigh about 100 grams, or around 4 ounces, and will be compensated for changes in temperature as pressure obviously varies with temperature. To be of real value the altimeter must be accurate and graduated to read to 10 metres or 30 feet. This will not enable you to locate your position to within 10 metres unless you are on a rock face. On a 25% slope, 1:4 or of 14 degrees, this would enable you to establish your position theoretically to within 40 metres, while on a slope of 30 degrees (scree slopes average around 36 degrees) you would be able to fix your position to around 20 metres. See Fig. 15.4. In practice other variables may influence the accuracy.

**FIG. 15.4**  Position on a line feature using an altimeter and ridge, spur, glacier or path

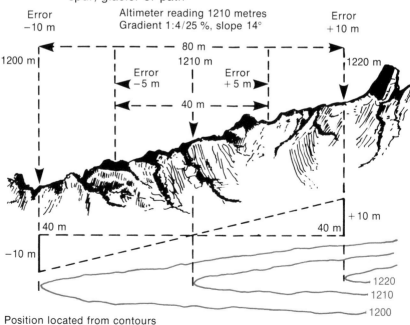

Position located from contours

Because there are two variables:

■ Your altitude.

■ The air pressure prevailing in a particular locality at a particular time.

it is impossible to use an altimeter or barometer without first setting the instrument by some external reference. The pilot of an aircraft normally has the advantage of being able to set the altimeter to the altitude above mean sea-level for a particular area (QNH), or of height above an aerodrome (QFE) by radio before landing. The mountaineer has no such facility and has to set his altimeter by means of the map. This echoes a theme of previous chapters where information is stored so that it can be utilized at some time in the future.

The altimeter is very simple to use. Before making an ascent or descent the instrument is set by turning the pointer needle by means of the knob to the altitude of your position. Your altitude may be determined from the contours on the map, or, more reliably, from a spot height— it would be wrong to assume that the contours on maps in various countries of the world have the same accuracy as you would expect from Ordnance Survey maps of this country. The needle will then read your altitude as your ascent or descent progresses and, by relating

*"In some places the altimeter may be more of a necessity than a luxury".*

**FIG. 15.5** Fixing position by altimeter and slope direction

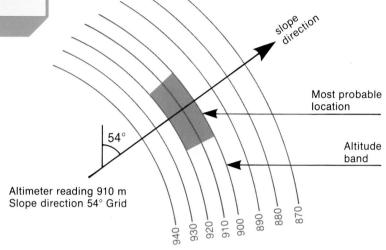

slope direction

Most probable
location

Altitude
band

54°

Altimeter reading 910 m
Slope direction 54° Grid

940 930 920 910 900 890 880 870

On a mountain flank the altimeter will establish position on a
height band. Used in conjunction with the compass to determine
slope direction it will enable position to be established with
reasonable accuracy even in limited visibility. (See FIG. 13.15)
Or, if totally lost, reduce the number of possible locations.

this altitude to the contours of your map, you will be able to establish
your position or at least obtain a position line.

On a line feature such as a spur, ridge, arête or glacier, the reading on
your altimeter should enable you to establish your position with
considerable accuracy, and usually to within a few tens of metres. On
the flank of a mountain it will give you a position line, but, if in
conjunction with the compass, the direction of the slope can be found,
it should be possible to fix your position from the two position lines
provided by the two instruments. This technique may be of
considerable use in restricted visibility as it is usually possible to
determine slope direction even in cloud. See Fig. 15.5 and refer to
Chapter 13. "More ways with the Compass." The altimeter is of great
assistance when contouring in both good and bad visibility. Contouring
is a technique which should be practised as it is a skill which not only
has obvious uses in difficult terrain, but is also an effective test of
proficiency with the instrument.

The barometric pressure varies not only with altitude but with the weather conditions prevailing in a locality and from place to place. We are all familiar with this from the synoptic charts, the pattern of isobars, which appear on television with the weather forecasts. The stable conditions of an anticyclone or high pressure system may not influence the reading of the altimeter significantly over several days and it may be necessary to travel many kilometres before any change of pressure is discernible; this is especially so when the pressure is above 1030 millibars (mb). During a depression, cyclone, or low pressure system, pressure can change quickly in a few hours and over a distance of a few kilometres and these changes can lead to errors of several, or many tens of, metres in the height indicated by the altimeter. Between the latitudes of 50 degrees and 60 degrees, where polar and tropical air meet, weather may seem to consist of an endless succession of depressions causing continuous changes in pressure. To avoid error every opportunity to reset the altimeter from the marked altitudes of places on your route should be taken. This is particularly important during unsettled weather conditions. On reaching a bivouac or campsite it is advisable to make a note of the altitude so that in the morning, if there has been a significant change in air pressure during the night, the altimeter can be reset to the altitude registered the night before which is more likely to be correct. A change of 1 mb in Mean Sea Level (MSL) pressure will give rise to an error of 10 metres in altitude. The Standard Atmosphere is 1013.25 mb at MSL at 15 degrees C. A pressure change of 1 mb over a couple of hours would not be unusual.

Your altimeter, since it is a very accurate barometer, has an equally important role as an aid to weather forecasting. When coupled with close observation of the cloud types and their sequence as well as noting changes in the direction of the wind, you have at your disposal the most effective method of predicting the onset of a depression and its associated bad weather, available to a person or group out of radio contact. But that is another story. By setting the altimeter needle to your altitude, the pressure at MSL can be read off the pressure scale opposite the zero on the altitude scale. It is not the absolute pressure

which is important however. It is the rise or fall of the barometer and the rate of change which is most significant. Movement in a clockwise direction indicates falling pressure while an anticlockwise movement means that the pressure is rising. A fall of 3 mb or more over a period of an hour would provide cause for concern as it would probably indicate a deep depression with high winds.

As with the compass, familiarity brought about by constant use is essential if the full potential of the altimeter is to be realized. Limitations are determined by the ability of the user rather than by the potential of the instrument. To use the altimeter effectively you must become a barometer watcher. You need to "have it around". Only by becoming totally familiar with its behaviour as a measurer of air pressure and its response to changing weather conditions can it serve as a navigational instrument which will enable you to find your altitude accurately and establish your location; possibly on that one vital occasion when you are not receiving much assistance from any other sources.

## SUMMARY

The skills of map and compass remain the same abroad, though the maps may differ and magnetic variation may be towards the East or West. In a large area of Europe the difference between True North and Magnetic North is so small that it is not worth bothering about and the map bearings may be transposed to the compass directly. When the magnetic variation is to the East the compensation is the opposite to that made in the British Isles.

Many foreign maps do not have any grid lines and the lines of longitude must be used instead. It may be necessary to draw parallel lines on the map in the area where you are travelling. More attention should be addressed to the marginal information and such detail as contour interval and whether it is the same for lowland and highland areas.

In Chapter 3, "Using the Map" we considered that the level of accomplishment in map reading required by navigators on land was to be able to select the most appropriate route between two places and then, using the information provided by the map, to be able to visualize and describe the route as if they were actually travelling along the route. This ability to map read may be compared directly with the process of learning to read English as infants. In the first year or so progress is slow and often laborious but then speed and fluency rapidly increase as vocabulary and, most importantly, experience and understanding expand.

The conventional signs, the contours, the representation of landforms are the vocabulary of map reading but they are not sufficient in themselves. Just as in learning to read English, it is essential that understanding, background knowledge and experience illuminate our reading and interpretation of the map. Nearly all who go into the mountains or wild country develop an interest in the countryside, and it is surprising how many who go into the hills purely for physical challenge initially, develop a lifelong interest and eventually identify strongly with the mountainous country in which they recreate. The more we learn about the country and the processes which have created our present landscape, the greater will be our ability to understand and interpret the map.

The nature of the underlying rock has the greatest influence on the landscape and in giving the characteristic shapes and outlines to the scenery. For example, limestone can nearly always give rise to dramatic scenery, whether in the Yorkshire Dales, the Dolomites, the Causses of Southern France, or in Yugoslavia. An understanding of any one of these regions will enable many of the features and characteristics of the landscape and scenery of the others to be anticipated and is of considerable help in understanding and interpreting the map. The outstanding scarp slopes, the scars, the dry valleys and the grikes are all on the map for the discerning eye to appreciate.

*"The isolated contour may represent a depression rather than a knoll".*

There is no need to travel abroad to appreciate the influence of geology on the landscape. The judicious selection of different parts of the country, each with its characteristic type of terrain, in which to practise route finding can hasten the acquisition of experience and understanding, especially if this is assisted by prior reading and study. Chalk and limestone are both slightly soluble in acid water and the isolated contour which would normally be interpreted as representing a small knoll may be found to represent the depression of a swallow or shake-hole where the water has found its way underground. The blue line on the map, which is so frequently the characteristic of a valley, is often absent in chalk and limestone areas and the broad escarpments which are associated with these rocks whether on the Downs or the North of England become familiar, as does the distinctive flora and the short springy turf which is such a delight to walk on.

259

Frequently, the change in terrain brought about by changes in the underlying geology is clear and abrupt whether this be in igneous or sedimentary rocks. Even the casual observer in Borrowdale cannot fail to notice the difference between the wild rugged grandeur created by the Borrowdale Volcanic Series and the gentle and rounded summits of the more easily weathered Skiddaw Slates; and the walker will be well aware of the difference it makes to his progress even if the reason for the change cannot be accounted for. Similarly, the dramatic increase in speed of travel when transferring from the waterlogged, peat hags, cloughs, and tussocks of the sedimentary millstone grits to the well-drained short turf of the sedimentary limestone rocks cannot pass unnoticed.

To the observant eye, evidence of the underlying geology is all around. Rock is very heavy to move about, and while the rich land owner may have had the stone for his mansion brought from afar, all the vernacular architecture, buildings and the walls forming the field boundaries will have been collected from the land surface or quarried as near as possible to the place of use. The buildings, gate posts, walls and other structures are indicators of the underlying rock.

*"To the observant eye, evidence of the underlying geology is all around".*

The rocks have been sculpted and shaped by erosion and the scenery greatly influenced by man's occupation. It is necessary to search hard and long for original landscape in the British Isles though such areas do remain even if they may be only fragments of once larger areas. These areas are more likely to be found in upland areas, but even in the uplands the effects of his grazing animals on the flora must never be underestimated. Deforestation over many centuries, followed by increasingly effective drainage methods and liming in more recent times, have all had a profound effect on the upland landscape.

A most significant difference between the various regions of the British Isles is the effect that glaciation has had in shaping the landscape. It is necessary for all who wish to have a deeper understanding of topography to travel to areas which will extend their experience. This should not be a one-way process—to fully appreciate the nature of glaciated country it is necessary to have an awareness of country which has not been glaciated. To appreciate the unglaciated country South of the Thames/Severn, and compare the areas of the Midlands affected by ice sheets with the mountain glaciation of Wales, Scotland and the North of England. To see the processes of glaciation in action

*"Names locate position and often identify landforms".*　　　　© *Crown copyright*

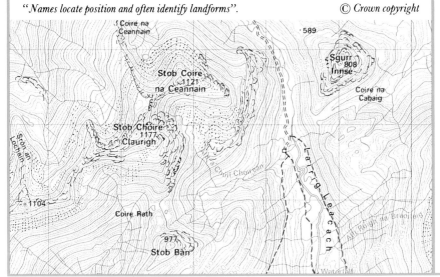

it will be necessary to travel abroad, perhaps to the Alps or Norway. In Scandinavia and the Alps the action of snow and ice can be seen at work carrying out the process of erosion and creating landforms, such as the cirques, arêtes, and hanging valleys to be found in the mountainous areas of Britain.

It would be wrong to assume that mountainous country is always the hardest to navigate in. The moorlands of our upland plateaux such as the Pennines, often present a greater navigational challenge. Certain lowland areas would present an even greater challenge to the route-finder if it were not for their thousands of years of habitation and use.

Areas of Devon and the Midlands spring to mind, where the soft sandstone or clays have resulted in a landscape consisting of an endless multitude of low rounded hills without any discernible pattern or grain. Even when viewed on the map, it is difficult to determine the drainage pattern or orient the country and on the ground it is well-nigh impossible; even the maze of country roads and lanes which meander through these areas, often with an apparent aimlessness, do not offer much assistance unless they are signposted.

The area around the Wash, like all low-lying areas where there are few vantage points to overlook the landscape, pose their own particular problems. The "main drains" and their tributaries form barriers to progress which are not discernible on the ground from any distance. Though the land may be flat and featureless, it still has a pronounced "grain" or orientation determined by the canalized drainage pattern which dictates the direction of road, track or path and therefore of travel. Such areas are common abroad as well as in this country, and all present similar problems to those who wish to find their way off the beaten track.

The names on the map not only indicate a particular location but they frequently give a strong clue to the landforms and the nature of the terrain. Our ancestors, whether they spoke Welsh, Gaelic, Anglo-Saxon, Danish or Norse all used simple descriptive names for the country and its features which are as applicable today as when they

262

*"To see glaciation in action it will be necessary to travel abroad".*

were first applied. We can still appreciate and delight in their sensitivity to colour, form and mood. No use of the maps of Wales or Scotland is complete without the presence of the Ordnance Survey's *Place names on the maps of Scotland and Wales*.

As mentioned previously, there is no English equivalent for cwm or coire (though the latter has been anglicized to corrie). In the Lake District "cove" is sometimes used as a substitute, though it has a different meaning and relates to different features in the South of England. Often the problem of a lack of a name for the feature is solved by just referring to the tarn which is so frequently associated with the corrie. Local names for landforms and features are commonplace and are often helpful in anticipating the nature of the landscape and its features.

There are other obvious ways of extending our understanding of the map and increasing its usefulness for planning ventures in unfamiliar country. A visit to any local library will reveal a vast range of guides and descriptive material for any part of the country and for every continent. Much of this material was conceived with the traveller in mind.

263

There are a number of monthly magazines catering for the needs of the climber, mountaineer, rambler and those who take their recreation in the outdoors. These magazines are illustrated with excellent photographs of all parts of this country, Europe and the world. When used in conjunction with the map they can often provide a very effective photographic reconnaissance for future expeditions. They can reveal considerable detail about conditions underfoot, the underlying geology, the landforms and the difficulty of the terrain. It is frequently possible to work out lines of approach or discern feasible routes, and many successful first ascents have been made from photographs with much less quality and detail than those which appear regularly in these monthly magazines.

There are other ways of supporting the map and gaining an understanding of an area. It may be helpful when visiting unfamiliar country to pin up a small scale map in such a place where it will be in constant view. A "Quarter Inch to the Mile" would serve the purpose well because the layer colouring of the contours gives a very strong impression not only of the relief but of the grain of the land as well. Over a period of a few weeks it is possible to acquire a considerable familiarity with the outstanding features and their relationship with each other, and of the general orientation of the landscape which may not be so apparent from the larger scale map which will be used during the venture.

## SUMMARY
The map will always remain the basic instrument of route-finding and navigation on land, but no effort should be spared in supplementing the information provided by the map, through the use of other sources. Only by increasing the breadth of our knowledge and the depth of our understanding can we extract all the information and detail which the cartographer has so painstakingly bestowed upon our maps to enable us to travel purposefully, or wander confidently in strange lands.

# APPENDICES

# Appendix 1

## Measuring Scales

### Romer

Usually it is sufficient to estimate the third and sixth figure of a Grid Reference by the eye, but since they are a means of communication it is sometimes necessary to be more precise—there may be two or more similar features in the same area. A romer is a scale which measures Grid References. It is marked off in units of a hundred metres reading from right to left and from top to bottom. It is simple to make, using the corner of a piece of card or paper using the grid subdivisions on the border of a map. Obviously a different romer is needed for each scale of map and there is only need for nine units.

The corner is placed against the feature in question and the third figure of the Easting is read off against the previous grid line to the left, while the Northing, the sixth figure, is read off against the grid line below. To be accurate, unless a feature is actually on the line, the lower figure should be used—not the nearest. There is a romer for both the 1:25000 and the 1:50000 scale maps on the opposite sides of the scale illustrated.

### Distance Scales

Measuring distances on a map is usually performed by means of a piece of thin string or a piece of paper and then transferring it to the linear scale on the map border. This process can be simplified and speeded up by marking out a distance scale on a piece of card or plastic. Scales have been marked out for the 1:25000 scale maps on one side of the scale shown in the illustration, while on the other side there is a scale for the 1:50000 *Landranger* maps. Using such a scale distances can be read directly from the map, either as the crow flies, or by following the bends of a path. It is of considerable assistance in route planning and improving one's ability to estimate distance by the eye.

### Time Scales

Since the measurement of distance is usually just a means to an end—that of determining journey time—further assistance is provided on the scale by including two time scales for both the 1:25000 and the 1:50000 scale maps directly below the distance scales. The scale nearest to the distance scale, coloured blue, is for walkers without a pack travelling at 5 kilometres per hour or about 3 miles per hour.

The lower scale, coloured red, is for walkers with a pack travelling at 4 kph or 2 mph. Using these scales it is possible to read journey times directly off the map which is a great help when using the map out of doors or when route planning. Admittedly it is not a personalized scale but with a little practice you should find it of considerable assistance, especially where groups of people are involved.

## Pacing Scale

A pacing scale has also been included. Its range is 500 metres. This scale just gives the average number of paces required. This is the scale which you will most probably need to personalize. Calculate the number of double paces, right foot to right foot or left to left, you need for a hundred metres. Personalize the scale by covering the numbers on the scale with white opaque typewriter fluid and then writing on the number of paces you require, using a waterproof ball point pen, or cover with adhesive paper. (See Chapter 8 Pacing).

## Contour Counter

The steepness or gradient of a slope is most easily determined by how closely the contours are spaced on the map. On the edge of the scale opposite to the distance scale a "Contour Counter" has been included which should enable you to determine the gradient of a slope in a matter of seconds once you are familiar with its use. The counter is designed for maps with a vertical or contour interval of 10 metres and again there is one for the 1:25000 map on one side and another for the 1:50000 on the other. Look closely at the white measures between the black spacers and you will notice that the measures are not all of the same size and that there is no apparent sequence in the numbers. When you have a moment to spare you can work out why this is so but in the meantime be content that I have made the calculations. The measures cover the more significant gradients between 10% (1 in 10) and 67% (1 in 1.5). The steeper gradients are to the right hand of the scale while the measures for the less steep are to the left. Using your 1:25000 map of an upland area, where the contour interval is 10 metres, choose an area where the contours are evenly spaced. Select a measure near to the centre of the scale and place the left side of the measure against a contour and then count the number of contours to the other side of the measure. If there are more contours than the number marked in the measure, slide the scale across the map to a steeper gradient; if there are not enough, move to a less steep gradient. The contour against the left mark does not count as you are really counting the number of spaces between the contours and you always

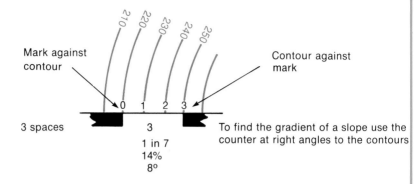

Mark against contour

Contour against mark

3 spaces

3
1 in 7
14%
8°

To find the gradient of a slope use the counter at right angles to the contours

The contour against the left hand mark does not count as you always need one more line to contain a given number of spaces

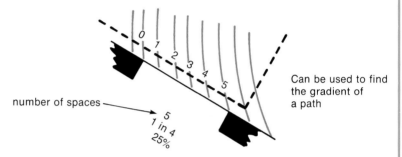

number of spaces

5
1 in 4
25%

Can be used to find the gradient of a path

On 1:50000 maps the spaces between thick contours (50 metre Vertical interval) will have to be used on the steeper slopes
On the 1:25000 maps thick contours will have to be used at a gradient of 67% (1 in 1.5) and probably at 50% (1 in 2)

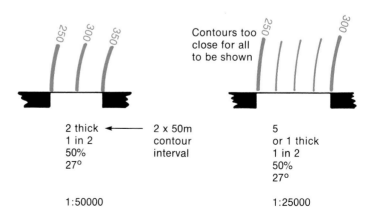

2 thick        ◄——  2 x 50m
1 in 2                contour
50%                  interval
27°

Contours too close for all to be shown

5
or 1 thick
1 in 2
50%
27°

1:50000

1:25000

need one extra line to contain a given number of spaces. Repeat if necessary until you find a measure where the number of contours on the map coincides (or most nearly coincides) with the number in the measure.

In Chapter 6, Gradients, it was stated that in the representation of steep slopes on the map, the contours may be so close together that lengths of some contours, usually the intermediate ones between every fifth thick contour, have to be deleted. Using the 1:25000 Contour Counter should present few problems for, at the gradients in question, all the contours will usually be on the map, though at gradients of 50% (1:2) and 67% (1:1.5) it is often more convenient to use the distance between two thick contours. On the 1:50000 map at gradients of 50% all the intermediate contours may or may not be shown so the distance between two thick contours should be used. At a gradient of 67% intermediate contours will have been deleted so you will need to relate the counter to the two space between three thick contours.

A gradient of 50% will indicate the need to zig-zag, especially if you are backpacking. A gradient of 67% with its angle of 34 degrees brings you within three or four degrees of the angle of the average scree scope and walking changes to scrambling, when care is essential in picking and choosing your route.

Using maps of mountainous areas, starting with an *Outdoor Leisure* map, practise relating the contours to the measures and the measures to the contours. Once you are familiar with the process you will move almost instinctively to the correct measure. The gradient is expressed as a percentage, as a ratio and as an angle. The counter is equally effective in finding the maximum gradient of a slope or the gradient of a path running obliquely or zig-zagging across a slope. The counter cannot, of course, measure the infinity of differing gradients but you will be able to interpolate with a little practice and experience. If the Contour Counter is used in lowland areas with the 1:25000 maps where the contour or vertical interval is 5 metres just double the number of contours within each measure.

The Counter should not only assist in your appreciation of gradient but be useful in route planning as it may help in deciding where you can and cannot go; whether this be determined by equipment, competence, confidence or simply physical stamina. You may also find it an interesting exercise to determine the gradients of sections of footpaths which are household names.

# Appendix 2

## The National Grid

In Chapter 3, "The Preparatory Skills", we noted that a six-figure grid reference would normally meet all our needs. Estimation by the eye is usually sufficient but if precision is necessary we can use a romer (see Appendix 1). If a grid reference does not seem to make sense it is always worth while changing the first 3 figures for the second three: e.g. 123456 becomes 456123 just in case the provider placed the Northings before the Eastings.

A grid reference taken from a map marked with the National Grid can be found on any other map marked with the National Grid whether it be at a scale of 1:25000, 1:50000, a One Inch to the Mile *Tourist Map* or a motoring atlas. Though six figure grid references are repeated every 100 kilometres (about 62 miles) this does not cause confusion in practice, but there are times when we wish to make them unique. If you consider a map of the National Grid you will see that each 100 kilometre square is identified by two letters—if these letters are placed in front of a six figure grid reference it will become unique e.g. SD942771. The appropriate letters will be found on your map in the marginal information. If you wish to arrange a meeting place with others, even at the opposite end of the country, all that is required is to prefix the six figures with the appropriate two letters and they will be able to locate the position on any scale of map they have available, providing that it is marked with the National Grid.

The projection on which the National Grid is based is a modified Transverse Mercator with its true origin at 2 degrees West, 49 degrees North. To avoid having negative references to the West of the 2 degrees West meridian and the North of Scottish mainland exceeding 1000 kilometres from the point of origin, all the distances are measured East and North from a false origin 49° 46′N, 7° 33′W, just South and to the West of the Scilly Isles. The grid line on the meridian 2 degrees West coincides with True North. Grid lines to the East and West diverge slightly from true North but this divergence is never great because mainland Britain is a "tall thin" country and even in Norfolk, Cornwall and the West of Scotland the maximum divergence is only about 3 degrees.

# Appendix 3

## Direction

In Chapter 3 you were advised to relate direction to the cardinal and half-cardinal points because the routes and paths which usually control our travel wander about with continual changes of direction. As long as you know the general direction in which you are travelling, the name of that direction is of minor importance. If however you are a regular map user, and all those with whom you wish to communicate are competent as well, you can add another eight geographical directions to your repertoire; the "three letter" directions.

The rose of the mariner's compass had 32 points, the 16 mentioned above plus the 16 "by" points. The first quarter of the rose is shown below.

Being able to recite the 32 points of the compass was known as "boxing the compass". While these sailing points, as they were known, were necessary and adequate for a sailing ship, this does illustrate the need for you to keep things simple and avoid the confusion which may arise from over-complication.

The "Three-letter" directions

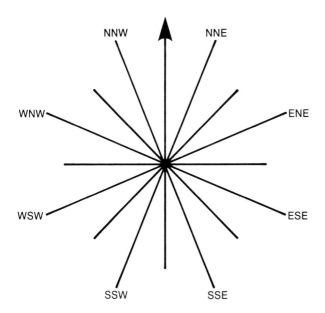

The "By-points" in the
first quarter

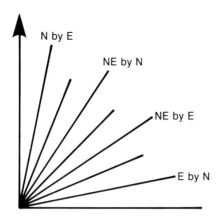

The potential for confusion is obvious

## Direction from the Stars

The Pole Star can be most easily located from the "pointers" in the constellation of the Great Bear or the Plough. Locate the distinctive pattern of the Great Bear which rotates around the Pole Star like the other stars and may be at any angle or even upside down. Using the distance between the pointers as a measure move up 5 lengths towards the zenith where you will find a fairly isolated bright star—the Pole Star. A closer look will reveal that it is the brightest star in the constellation of the Little Bear. The Great Bear never sets in the latitude of the British Isles but if it is obscured by cloud the constellation of Cassiopeia, with its characteristic "W" shape, on the opposite side of the Pole Star to the Great Bear can be of assistance. Roughly bisect the angle of the more open of the two "V"s and it will lead to the Pole Star. Cassiopeia is about the same distance from Polaris as the Great Bear, about 30 degrees. Polaris is very high in the sky in these latitudes so it is helpful to relate its direction and your direction of travel to some point on the outline, or loom, of the horizon—usually possible on a starlight night. Make the most of your opportunities to familiarize yourself with the star patterns of the night sky, especially around camp in wild country when the clear mountain air and darkness, unpolluted by city lights, reveal the heavens in their full glory.

# Appendix 4

## Finding direction from the Sun and a Watch

If the sun is visible and you have a watch it is possible to establish roughly the North-South line. Take the watch off your wrist and lay it on a flat surface. During the winter months when Greenwich Mean Time (GMT) is in use, turn the watch round until the hour hand is pointing at the sun—South is halfway between the hour hand and twelve o'clock. During British Summer Time (BST) point the hour hand at the sun in the same way but South will be halfway between the hour hand and ONE O'CLOCK. This is better than adjusting your watch to GMT, you may forget to reset your watch and you may lose the time as well as your direction. In other countries the watch must be set to local time.

In the southern hemisphere twelve o'clock should be pointed towards the sun; NORTH will lie halfway between the hour hand and twelve o'clock. It does not matter if your watch is not very accurate because the method is not very accurate for reasons stated in Chapter 15. If your watch is digital draw a clock face on a piece of paper or on anything to hand.

Finding direction by the sun and a watch

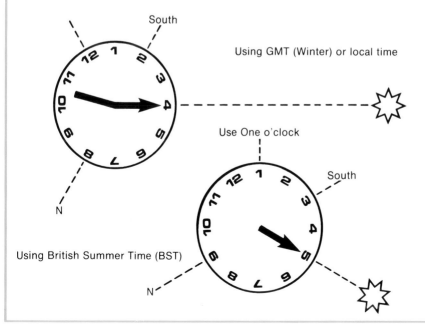

Using GMT (Winter) or local time

Use One o'clock

Using British Summer Time (BST)

**Wild Country Expedition Panel Areas in England, Wales and Northern Ireland.**

**Wild Country Expedition Panel Areas in England, Wales and Northern Ireland.**

**Northern Ireland**

18   Sperrin Mountains (also Co. Fermanagh and Co.

Donegal)

19   North Antrim Hills and Antrim Plateau

20   Mourne Mountains

**England**

21   Isle of Man

22   Cumbria (Lake District)

23   Cheviots (Cheviot Hills, Border Forests)

24   High Pennines & Durham Dales (Teesdale, Weardale,

Allendale and West to Cross Fell)

25   North Yorkshire (South Teeside to Wenslydale)

26   Yorkshire Dales (Langstrothdale to South Pennines)

27   North York Moors (North York Moors & Cleveland Hills)

28   Peak District

32   Dartmoor

**Wales**

29   Snowdonia

30   Mid Wales

31   Beacons X

**Wild Country Expedition Panel Areas in Scotland**

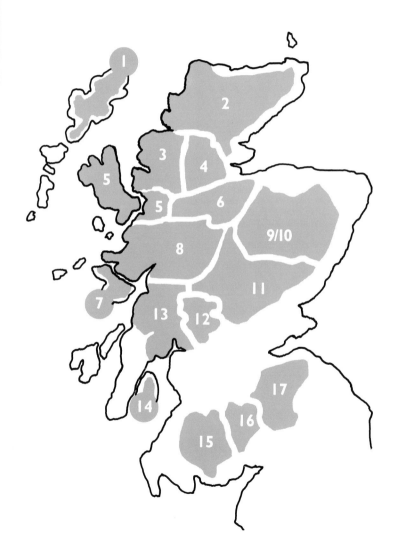

## Wild Country Expedition Panel Areas in Scotland

**Scotland**

1    Western Isles

2    Caithness & Sutherland

3    Wester Ross

4    Easter Ross

5    Isle of Skye & Lochalsh

6    Inverness

7    Isle of Mull

8    Lochaber & District

9/10 Grampian & Cairngorm

11   Tayside

12   Trossachs & Crianlarich

13   Lomond & Argyl

14   Isle of Arran

15   Galloway Hills

16   Lowther Hills

17   Scottish Borders

Also in Germany
Bavaria Panel (BA)

## The Duke of Edinburgh's Award
## Wild Country Expedition Panels

**In the United Kingdom** The foregoing areas are defined as wild country by the Award Scheme and the Mountain Walking Leader Training Board. In each area there is a voluntary Expedition Panel to advise on all aspects of Award ventures being undertaken there. Names and addresses of all the Panel Secretaries are published on the Award Scheme staff list circulated every January in the *Award Journal*. **Advance notice (in duplicate on the Standard *Expedition Notification Form* available through all Operating Authorities) must be given of all ventures (including practise journeys) going into these areas at least six weeks before hand or four weeks if no assessor is required, addressed to the appropriate Panel Secretary.** Certain Award operators, e.g. Outward Bound schools may, however, negotiate blanket agreements with the panels on an annual basis to avoid the need for rendering forms for each individual expedition, practice journey or training exercise. Further details are available from Award Offices.

**In winter** (i.e., between November and March inclusive) particular care is to be taken in connection with any venture in wild country. The headquarters of the Operating Authorities concerned, or their authorized delegates, are to give approval, in writing, for any such venture before it is undertaken and the plans **must** be agreed with the wild country Expedition Panel for the area being visited. If snow and ice are likely to be encountered, ventures may only be undertaken by expert organizations.

It is expected that supervisors of groups undertaking expeditions in the close season will be qualified to Winter Mountain Leader level or have equivalent experience, and that participants involved in such expeditions will generally be over 17 years of age as the time after entering the Gold Award, at their sixteenth birthday, will have been spent gaining wild country experience in the summer months.

**Aiming Off**   Intentionally planning a course which will lead to one side of an intended objective which lies on a line or collecting feature to avoid the uncertainty of not knowing which way to turn if the objective is not in sight. The objective must lie on a collecting feature.

**Alternative Route**   A planned route, usually for use in difficult conditions, which will enable the intended destination to be reached; usually by going "round" or "through" rather than "over" and so avoiding the restricted visibility of cloud, the full force of the wind, or ice and snow. Alternative routes frequently follow line features which simplify navigation in restricted visibility (see ESCAPE ROUTE).

**Arête**   A knife edge ridge found between two cirques frequently with a sharp serrated edge.

**Attack Point**   An easily located landmark or feature nearer to the objective which will simplify the problems of route finding and location, usually by reducing the distance required to be travelled on a compass bearing.

**Back Bearing**   A reciprocal bearing; a bearing to which 180 has been added or subtracted; a bearing obtained by bringing the white, or South seeking end of the compass needle to the "N" on the compass housing, resulting in a bearing exactly opposite to the original direction of travel. The reciprocal of a bearing taken on a landmark which is plotted from the landmark back to the observer to provide a position line. (The back bearing must be adjusted to compensate for magnetic variation if plotted on a map.)

**Back Tracking**   Retracing a route or path relying on the carefully observed details of landmarks and features noted on the outward journey to enable the path to be followed on the way back.

**Cirque**   (Corrie, coire, cwm) A deep rounded hollow or basin in a mountainside or at a valley head formed though the erosion by snow and ice. They often have a characteristic armchair shape where the back wall is a steep cliff. The side walls may be steep cliffs terminating in arêtes. Old cirques may have a tarn or lake in the bottom. There is no exact English equivalent so cwm or corrie is usually used according to location.

**Col**   A pass or saddle between two hills or mountains; a depression in a range of hills or mountains which provides access between one valley and another.

**Combe**  (Coombe, Coomb) A small valley in a hillside, usually with rounded grassy slopes frequently found in chalk areas.

**Contour**  A line drawn on a map joining all places at the same height above sea level.

**Contouring**  Following a route which maintains a constant height. A route which goes round the head of a steep valley or ravine rather than descending and then climbing up the other side, or travelling round high ground rather than climbing over it.

**Corrie**  Anglicized form of the Gaelic Coire. See CIRQUE.

**Cove**  A small inlet or creek but occasionally used as a substitute for cirque e.g. Nethermost Cove.

**Cwm**  The Welsh word for a cirque. See CIRQUE.

**Dead Reckoning**  Reaching an objective by travelling in the required direction on a compass bearing for the requisite distance. A cornerstone of classical navigation which still has a limited role on land in featureless terrain or restricted visibility.

**Dip Slope**  The more gentle slope of an Escarpment.

**Edge**  The junction between two upward slopes. An arête e.g. Striding Edge; a cuesta or escarpment e.g. Wenlock Edge; a rocky outcrop e.g. Froggatt Edge.

**Escape Route**  A route which enables escape from difficult or dangerous conditions. Usually it leads to lower ground to avoid restricted visibility, the full force of the weather, or ice and snow. Unlike an ALTERNATIVE ROUTE it may not enable the original destination to be reached and may only bring about a temporary alleviation of problems.

**Escarpment**  A ridge which has a steep, or scarp, slope on one side and a gentle, or dip, slope on the other. Escarpment is sometimes applied to the scarp slope alone but never to the dip slope alone.

**Fix**  A position obtained by means of bearings. See Resection, Position Lines.

**Gill**  (Ghyll) An upland stream, or the depression containing a stream. The word is used throughout the North of England but particularly in the Dales and the Lake District. It may be a small or major feature or an alternative name for a gully.

**Gully**   A narrow channel, or cleft cut into a hill or mountainside by water and ice. Frequently contains waterfalls and pitches. Provides excellent sport for scramblers and climbers but can be wet, slippery and dangerous for the descending walker.

**Hanging Valley**   A tributary valley which enters the main valley well above the valley floor. Often found in glaciated regions but may occur elsewhere where the main valley has been eroded more quickly than the tributary valley. The river or stream of the hanging valley may enter the main valley by spectacular waterfalls or torrents.

**Line or Linear Feature**   A feature, natural or man-made, which has length and can therefore provide direction for the navigator. It may just provide orientation or it may be utilized as a route across the ground e.g. road, valley or ridge.

**Névé**   (and German Firn) The compacted and altered snow and granular ice which lies permanently in the cirques and snowfields of high mountains. Where the névé feeds glaciers it is gradually transformed into glacier ice.

**Orient, Orientate**   (verb) To set the map; to "get one's bearings", to identify the direction of the principal features in the landscape. From the Latin oriens orientis, the rising (of the sun), the East, which was the prime direction up to and during medieval times. Orientate is the back form of the verb developed from the noun but is equally acceptable. See SET.

**Orient**   (noun) The East.

**Pass**   A low, or the lowest, gap in a barrier of hills or mountains used for travel. See COL or SADDLE.

**Pinpoint**   To locate position accurately by proximity to landmarks or point features.

**Plateau**   An area of high level, or nearly level ground. It may be a small local feature or as large as Tibet. Plateaux exist in many forms under different names and are frequently dissected by valleys.

**Point Feature**   A landmark or spot feature marked on the map which will assist in the accurate establishment of position.

**Position Line**   A compass bearing taken on a landmark which is then converted to a back bearing and drawn on the map from the landmark towards the observer; the observer's location will be somewhere along the line. Position lines form the basis of finding position by RESECTION. A position line may also be obtained from two landmarks in transit; an observer will be located on a line drawn through the two points towards the observer.

**Re-entrant**  A subsidiary or side valley; the area of lower ground between two spurs. The term is often applied to a depression which does not justify the use of the word valley.

**Resection**  Fixing position by means of two or more position lines obtained from compass bearings. See POSITION LINES.

**Ridge**  The junction between two upward slopes. It may be narrow with steep cliffs or broad and well rounded. Ridges may lead to or connect mountain summits.

**Saddle**  A depression in a range of hills or between two summits which facilitates travel between two valleys. The English equivalent of Col.

**Scarp**  (Scarp slope) The steep slope of an escarpment. An inland line of cliffs.

**Set**  (To set the map) to turn the map round until the direction of the features and landmarks on the map coincide with the direction of the features in the landscape from the observer's position. To turn the map round until the North of the map is in the direction of True North. To orientate the map.

**Spur**  A well-rounded ridge of a hill or mountain which extends into lower ground.

**Swallow, Sink, Pot or Shake Hole**  A hollow or depression in limestone or chalk areas where water enters, or has entered the ground to follow an underground course. Often represented on the map by a single contour, can easily be mistaken for a knoll.

**Tarn**  A small upland or mountain lake frequently found in a cwm or corrie. A Norse word used in the North of England. Compare with the Welsh Llyn or Ffynnon and the Gaelic Lochan.

**Track**  (verb) To follow progress across the country on the map by regularly pinpointing position by the landmarks and features encountered on the route.

**Truncated Spur**   A spur which has been partly cut away by glacial action which may result in it terminating in a steep or precipitous slope.

**Watershed**   The divide or high ground separating the headwaters of two different rivers or river systems.

# Bibliography

*Follow the Map.* An Ordnance Survey Guide. John G Wilson.
ISBN 0-7136-2459-0

*Place names on maps of Scotland and Wales.* The Ordnance Survey,
Southampton.

*Mountaincraft and Leadership.* Eric Langmuir. The Scottish Sports
Council and the Mountainwalking Leader Training Board.
ISBN 0-903908-75-1

*Mountain Navigation.* Peter Cliff. ISBN 0-904405-48-6

*Heading for the Scottish Hills.* Compiled by the Mountaineering Council
of Scotland and the Scottish Landowners' Federation.
ISBN 0-907521-24-X

*Out in the Country.* Countryside Commission. John Dower House,
Crescent Place, Cheltenham, Glos. GL50 3RA

*Tread Lightly.* British Mountaineering Council. Crawford House,
Precinct Centre, Booth Street East, Manchester M13 9RZ

The Royal Geographical Society, 1 Kensington Gore, Kensington,
London, has probably the largest private collection of maps in the
World. The use of the Map Room facilities are available to the public
by prior arrangement. Tel. 01-589-5466

## Photo Credits

The following photographers are gratefully credited for their work which appears on the pages listed below;

| | Page |
|---|---|
| Jim Gregson | 14, 40, 44, 89, 90, 95, 111, 112, 149, 163, 167, 177, 182, 187, 193, 195, 200, 203, 205, 235, 242, 245, 253, 259, 263, 279. |
| Lake District National Park Authority | 19, 29, 41, 42, 55, 70, 91, 98, 102, 119, 125, 136, 148, 173, 188, 218, 257. |
| Mike Blisset | 4, 13, 31, 58, 67, 73, 78, 83, 86, 127, 137, 144, 147, 207. |
| Wally Keay | 15, 39, 51, 57, 113, 122, 154, 169, 184, 243, 260. |
| Roy Rich | 25, 288. |
| Stuart Robertson | 194. |
| Roger Dixon | 265. |
| Bill Marshall | 175. |
| Deb Dowdall | 21. |
| Andreas Amling | 237. |

Front cover photographs by Matthew Roberts (Trailwalker Magazine) and back cover photograph by permission of The Lake District National Park.

# rdnance Survey
## maps for all walks of life

**vering the whole of Great Britain in detail,
ly Ordnance Survey maps help to open up
e whole country for you to explore.**

more information about
Inance Survey products and services

our **Customer Information HelpLine**

08456 05 05 05 and quote reference A499

**nail:** custinfo@ordsvy.gov.uk

**b site:** www.ordsvy.gov.uk

...linking you to the real world

# WE
# HAVE THE
# CHALLENGE
# WHERE
# ARE YOU?

The Award Scheme is open to all young people aged 14-25
is a programme of leisure-time activities.  There are three le
of Award: Bronze, Silver and Gold, and each has four Sectio
Service, Expeditions, Skills and Physical Recreation, with a
additional Residential Project for those 'Going for Gold'

You can take part in the Award through many schools, you
clubs, places of work and uniformed youth organisations

## YOU DON'T HAVE TO BE 14-25 TO BENEF
## FROM THE CHALLENGE OF THE AWARD.

Volunteer leaders and specialist instructors are always requ
by Award groups to help participants achieve their Awarc
You can give as little or as much of your time as you wish a
you do not need to have any experience of the Scheme

For further information on how you can be involved, eith
contact your local council or write to your local Territoria
Regional Officer.

Further copies of *Land Navigation*, as well as a catalogue o
Award items, are available from The Award Scheme Ltd,
Dublin Street, EDINBURGH, Scotland EH3 6NS.